THE FEMININE SOUL

Surprising Ways the Bible
Speaks to Women

JANET DAVIS

DEDICATION

This book is dedicated to the women whose stories are contained herein. Though, of course, your stories and names are disguised, you know who you are. You have inspired, informed, sustained, and mentored me well. Thank you.

> *Hear me heaven and earth,*
> *listen to what I say.*

> *May my thoughts fall like rain,*
> *may my words cling like dew.*

> *Like gentle rain upon tender grass,*
> *Like showers upon seedlings.*

> *I will praise the Lord's name,*
> *I will tell of God's greatness.*

> *Deuteronomy 32.1-3*[1]

CONTENTS

ACKNOWLEDGMENTS

For all of these ideas forever floating around in my head to be penned (and pinned!) to paper is a miracle wrought both by the unseen, mysterious hand of God and the very tangible hands (and arms and faces and voices) of the Body of Christ that grace my life. Thank you...

To my husband, Bob, who has given me the free space in which to grow.

To my children, Bobby, Jenna, and Betsy, who challenge and inspire me to great hope.

To my parents, Bill and Mary, who gave me a foundation that has held true and sure.

To my mentors, Marge, Patty, and Rita, who freely offer me womanly wisdom.

To my sisters of heart, Mary, Katy, Leslie, and Mary Ellen, who journey with me.

To my writer's group, Kathie, Lisa, Jamie, Theresa, and Wanda, with whom I share this success.

To my friend Matt who patiently answered countless Text questions, nudging me toward a fuller perspective.

To my counselors and professors, Ken, Don, Liam, Heather, Kirk, Dan, Brian, Beth, and Leighton who urged me to voice.

To dear friends, Sherry, Missy, Christie, and Carol who stir me up to good works.

To the members of my parish, St. Stephen's, Beaumont, who love me well.

To, Michael and Peter, Benedictine monks who provide refreshment for me... body, mind, and soul.

OTHER BOOKS by Janet Davis:

Sacred Healing: MRIs, marigolds, and miracles
(Twenty-third Publications, 2010)

My Own Worst Enemy: How to Stop Holding
Yourself Back
(Bethany House, spring 2012)

INTRODUCTION

Uniquely Feminine Spirituality

Spirituality is not unisex. Through the stories of women in Scripture, God invites us to rediscover our uniquely feminine experience of Him. With greater self-awareness, we can repent more effectively, grow more efficiently, and minister more powerfully.

~

THE problem with having an "aha" moment in a Starbucks coffee shop is that you cannot immediately determine if the source of your inspiration was the Spirit of God or a caffeine rush. Such was the case for me when it first dawned on me that women might have a remarkably unique, a distinctively *feminine*, Christian spirituality.

I was sitting with five friends between classes at Western Seminary– Seattle, where I was pursuing a master's degree in spiritual nurture. We were a bit of a motley crew. There were three men and three women. One lived in a houseboat on a river, one in a mansion on a hill. One was a grandmother. There were a couple of folks bringing up the middle—middle age, middle management, and middle income. I was forty years old, married, and the mother of three children.

As we sat and visited on a cool and wet (of course!) day, the men began to talk about the importance of words in their relationship with God. They spoke of Scripture, journaling, books, and so forth. Language defined and dominated their spirituality.

The more I listened, the more I realized that it wasn't the same for me. Certainly Scripture was of central and critical import to me, but it was far from my only source of learning, inspiration, and connection. For years I had been a gardener, and God had spoken to me time and again through nature. My experience of laboring and birthing children had also impacted my spiritual life profoundly. So I spoke up.

"Guys, I hear what you're saying, but it's just not like that for me. I relate to God in a much, much broader way."

"Say more," they invited.

"Well, this is probably just my particular quirkiness, but I almost see Scripture as the skeleton, providing form and structure and some boundaries, but there is a lot of flesh on those bones—the stuff of real life, things I can taste and touch and experience. I connect with God in those things, too."

As I continued to describe my different sense of spirituality, the other two women immediately chimed in with similar thoughts. Then it happened, that big "aha" moment.

"Maybe women have a whole different way of experiencing God than men." (I did finally conclude it was the Spirit of God because I was still on my first nonfat, half-caf, venti latte.)

Now, on one level this statement seems profoundly obvious—duh, of course we're different. Pharmaceutical companies know that. The folks at Harvard know it. We all know it.

On the other hand, have you ever heard a sermon addressing or even acknowledging that men and women differ spiritually? Have you ever seen different growth paradigms put forth for the different sexes? Has anyone in your church ever talked about how men and women sin differently? If they have, you attend a very unusual church. Most of us assume that spirituality is unisex.

My "aha" moment planted just the seed of a thought in my head, a hypothesis of sorts. Intuitively, I sensed that if this statement were true, the implications for me personally and the church as a whole would be huge. It wasn't something to be thrown around or suggested lightly.

As I began to carry that seed of a thought with me to class, to Scripture, and into my life, it began to grow. One of my first formal efforts at exploring the topic was a paper I wrote titled "The Nature of a Woman's Voice." Using the stories of women in Scripture, I made observations about how women tend to communicate most effectively. I was surprised by how much wisdom I found in those stories, a kind of uniquely *feminine* wisdom that began to change the way I lived.

It became more and more obvious to me that there are easily observable differences between the spirituality of the men and that of the women in Scripture. God said in Genesis that we were made male and female in God's image (see 1:27). Maybe He was really serious about that core-level uniqueness. Spurred by such a clear statement of essential difference, I began to look again at the Bible through a gender-specific lens.

One of the most important tools we have for the interpretation of Scripture is Scripture itself. I think the Bible writers were up to more than we think. Its multifaceted nature is the reason so much of Scripture was written in story form. I began to realize that the kinds of things my eyes and mind saw as I intentionally read Scripture *as a woman* had been missed by many who had taught me well in my years of study. I believe this oversight occurred simply because the Text wasn't read with an understanding of the feminine soul—specifically, where women struggle, how women grow, and how women reflect the glory of God. When you learn from life where the points of struggle, growth, and glory are, it is amazing how easily you can see them addressed and reflected in the Text and, as a result, can be educated and encouraged by observations that may not be conventional but are nevertheless valid.

As I continued to study, I was surprised—no, make that stunned—by what I found. For example, I noticed that though Jesus often rebuked His disciples and the Pharisees, He never rebuked women. Instead, He wooed and drew out women, using penetrating personal insight and positive affirmation to move them toward repentance. Though He often steered the male disciples away from ideas of self-importance, He moved women in the opposite direction, toward a greater sense of self. Though the male disciples struggled to hear the teachings of their Rabbi, the women in His world heard His message but sometimes struggled to learn to speak up.

As I explored the Old Testament, I found similar differences. God was repeatedly working to draw out and highlight these amazing women in gender-specific ways. In fact, it was the consistency in God's works with women in both the Old Testament and the New that impressed me the most. The persistent direction of growth for women was away from invisibility, smallness, and a narrow view of their feminine souls toward a remarkable, large, and memorable presence in God's kingdom. That consistency validated for me in a powerful way the critical importance of gender-specific spiritual growth for women.

Over the years, I have spoken to women of all ages in a vast array of life circumstances who have struggled to live wisely and at peace with their tender and powerful feminine souls. Could it be that this struggle is rooted deeply in the very shape of our souls? Might it be connected at an even deeper level than our experiences, however healthy or unhealthy they might be? Could there be something in the shape of our feminine souls that tends toward self-depreciation more than self-importance? Perhaps there is something about our greater awareness of the world and the people around us that bends us away from appropriate self-care. Maybe our noble tendency to nurture and care for others creates within us a vulnerability to the loss of our sense of self. Might our broader, more encompassing way of experiencing life cause us to lose track of ourselves in the midst of a rich and full daily existence? Most men do not struggle in these same ways.

Raising such questions is complicated by the fact that many women live for years unaware of their own pain. Do you see the Catch-22? Lack of awareness of our feminine souls both causes and covers the pain! Such was my experience.

Five years before my Starbucks "aha" moment, God had begun to do a revolutionary and healing work in my life—despite the fact that I was entirely unaware that anything in my life needed healing! From all I could see, my life was going well. Though a bit frustrated that God had given me three preschoolers to raise rather than the corporate executive job I thought better suited my giftedness, I was making the most of my days. I was a real duty-driven machine, accomplishing great things for God. In fact, I was quite proud of my seemingly emotionless ability to be competent and productive. Yet from somewhere deep inside my soul, an uninvited shift was beginning. This crisis was born from within, more like an earthquake than a hurricane.

In the course of trying to figure out what in the world was the matter with me, I spent hours reading, journaling, and meeting with a counselor. I began to realize that the person I had always perceived myself to be was simply a shell, an image I had used to encapsulate my entire life, seeking to protect my real self from exposure. Though I had pretended for years to be a duty-driven machine, in reality, I was a woman with a feminine soul who was very afraid and in much pain.

In my mid-thirties, sadly my pain and fear were *all* I knew of my feminine soul. The most terrifying part of that season was that I had so little idea of who I was. All my previous assumptions were now in question. It was a season of insight and deep personal challenge, much of which is recounted elsewhere in this book. The healing of my feminine soul that began in such pain and turmoil continued as I entered seminary five years later. In that nurturing environment, I first learned to speak my truth as a woman. And I first recognized the unique spirituality of the feminine soul.

After completing my master's degree and moving back to Texas, I began to enthusiastically explore the world of feminine spirituality, both within the church and without. I resonated with books on popular spirituality and feminism. They validated and fostered my new growth, as well as convinced me that the ache of a neglected feminine soul lives out in many shapes and forms. The circumstances may be different, but the pain is very similar. The growth paradigms I learned seemed more effective for me than those I had heard in the church. I drank in seminars and programs focused on empowering women. I joined women's groups. I pursued experiences that fostered my feminine spirituality. All these resources affirmed my uniqueness as a woman. There was a whole movement out there that seemed to know and understand me. Though at times I hesitated to admit it even to myself, this new path was definitely producing the fruit of God's Spirit in my life: love, joy, peace, patience, faithfulness, kindness, goodness, gentleness, and self-control.

Still, I could not escape the reality of my genuine spiritual growth in the church over many years. Even as I explored new avenues for growth, I continued in my study of Scripture. These two arenas of insight informed one another: Scripture lending needed guidance and boundaries, and the broader world of life experience offering new insights and lenses through which I could see even more in the Bible. I was continually surprised at how much of the feminine wisdom I had found outside the church could easily be seen in these stories recorded centuries ago! Though the church may have missed noticing gender-different spirituality, God had not missed writing it into that ancient sacred Book.

It is a simple matter of history that the primary source of understanding, interpretation, and teaching in the church has been the masculine voice. Certainly that voice has taught much truth to the church universal—important, critically soul-saving truth for both genders. Yet perhaps not all truths are gender neutral in understanding or application. Perhaps when men interpret the stories of women for women, they miss a thing or two. Perhaps when they seek to apply them to the lives of women, they lack the necessary insider perspective.

As I continued to study, I realized more and more that there are many precepts that live out differently in men and women. We sin differently, we grow differently, and we express God's glory differently. In fact, many of these differences are complementary, almost opposite in expression. At times, it felt as if I needed to walk backward, stand upside down on my head, or look in a mirror to observe them.

As I began to apply these new gender-specific insights to my life, my feminine soul began to grow and expand as never before. I was finally able to understand and let go of some long-standing self-destructive patterns. I finally found the courage to move forward with long-neglected dreams. On this path that fed my feminine soul uniquely, I felt the sun on my face and the wind in my hair. Even now, nearly fifteen years since this healing journey first began, my process of self-discovery continues.

The women of the Bible have mentored me along the way. Some became my friends as I sought initially to describe the nature of my feminine soul. Others taught me about uniquely feminine foibles and sins. Still others mentored me as I sought to grow, showing me what I needed and how to nurture my feminine soul. They helped me hear God's voice of calling and modeled for me the courage and faith required to respond obediently. These wise women have also given me eyes to see and a heart that values the unique giftedness of my feminine soul. Their stories form the substance of this book. If not for their influence in my life, I would never have had the vision to write or the courage to publish this work. I am forever in their debt.

What they have taught me, I now offer to you. In *The Feminine Soul*, you will be invited to discover in Scripture our uniquely feminine experience of God. Having spent most of my adult years in mainline evangelical churches, I have encountered many devout, Bible-believing women who have found themselves slowly dying in the midst of seeking to grow in their faith. Many run from study to study, good thing to good thing, seeking help with the unique struggles and aches in their hearts that no one in their spiritual community seems to effectively address. Most are busy; some are numb; a few are still seeking. Some live in awareness of their pain; for some it leaks out anytime they get still or sad. Their devotion at times becomes frustration, often showing up as depression, addiction (to a variety of things, including food), chronic disease, infidelity, unresolved grief, cynicism, or general malaise.

Like me, some of these struggling women will find their way to new personal growth through vehicles outside the church. They will find counselors, read books, listen to Oprah and Dr. Phil. Many will conclude that the life-affirming messages of popular spirituality and feminism cannot mix with their Christian faith. For the sake of the survival of their feminine souls, many will leave the church. Such departures are a tragic loss to these women and to the church; even more important, they are a reality God never intended and deeply grieves.

As I've held the cries of women (including my own) and our gathered stories alongside the stories of women in Scripture, I've noticed common themes. As I've connected with the deep, internal, and uniquely feminine struggles of these ancient women, I've also connected with God's healing presence in their lives. The more I study Scripture and the more I speak with women, the more convinced I am that awareness and nurturing of the feminine soul is a critically important issue in the spiritual lives of women. Whether we lose track of ourselves in busyness, caregiving, or shame, we need to hear the voice of God calling forth the truest and most feminine aspects of our nature, calling us as women to discover, embrace, grow, and serve with wisdom and peace from the depths of our feminine souls.

In society today, women everywhere are looking to other women for answers. Pick up almost any women's magazine in the grocery store and you will see articles on womanly getaways, girls' nights out, and feminine retreat options. Intuitively, we know that a central part of our current struggle in life has to do with the loss of our uniquely feminine wisdom and identity. What better source of wisdom and help could we seek out than Scripture? What wiser mentors than these ancient women of God?

I invite you to go back with me to our mentors of old: the women of the Bible. We will let Scripture interpret Scripture, let the lives of women living out God's truth define for us what those truths look like for women then and now.

In *Part One: Feminine Souls in Flight*, we will examine our gender-specific ways of running from God. Through the lives of ancient women struggling just like us, we will begin to see our affection for the seemingly safe yet deeply destructive choice to hide our feminine souls. We will observe how we can use both silence and words in ways that grieve God, hurt our souls, and distance ourselves from others. For too long we have played games and fled into busyness. We have been caught up in these uniquely feminine destructive patterns with little effective help. These women will begin to picture for us the pathway of uniquely feminine repentance and healing.

Part Two: Feminine Souls in Transition will explore the special challenges women face as we seek to grow. In these stories, we will see what a healthy, growing spiritual life looks like for women. We will be invited to overcome our passivity and actively listen for God's individual calling. We will examine the pathway to maturity, including the obstacles and helpful tools along the way. As we watch these women grow, we will discover how to make better choices that more effectively facilitate the growth of our feminine souls.

Finally, *Part Three: Feminine Souls in Service* celebrates a few of our gender's special gifts. We will observe the nature and power of the contributions of these women to God's work in the world. We will be invited to reexamine our often-dismissive perspective regarding some of our less culturally valued offerings. As we hear the voice of God elevating our feminine contributions, we will be inspired to embrace our unique giftedness with new passion.

These old stories are not the only ones you will be invited to explore in this book. Through questions that can be used for both personal reflection and small-group discussion, you will consider parts of your own story alongside both ancient and contemporary stories. As women, it is critical that we learn to confidently bring our feminine experience of the world to our reading of the Bible. It may be tempting for you to simply receive the voice of the author and the Scripture rather than taking the time to hear your own. I pray that you will choose a different way. Your voice and perspective are needed as we, together as a church, begin to unpack this huge arena of study.

You may find some questions deeply challenging and at times even painful to consider. For too long, we as women have not been effectively challenged because we have not been effectively known. I hope you will give yourself the freedom and essential time to converse with these thoughts and questions. They are designed to "plow up" the old, hard ground of long-standing and comfortable, but unhelpful, patterns. Do not expect that to be an easy task. As you meet these women and see God at work in their lives, my prayer is that you will open yourself to a new understanding of your own feminine soul and God's love for you.

These pages are full of good news. God sees us as women. God knows us and desires for us to grow. God nurtures our feminine souls, inviting us to be more and more who we were created to be. Some of these ancient women began their journeys as invisible women with painful, small, frustrated, misdirected, and narrow lives. As they responded to God's way in their lives, offering their unique gifts to the kingdom, their feminine souls were healed and grew in leaps and bounds. As they dared to be seen, to grow—indeed, to shine—they took their place in God's story and amazingly are still teaching us today. May God bless us with the same glorious transformation as we journey together.

Part One

FEMININE SOULS IN FLIGHT

CHAPTER ONE

Giving Up Silence, Daring to Speak

HANNAH IN 1 SAMUEL 1-2

As women, we encounter many painful elements in the world around us and within us that seek to silence us. We often surrender our voices early in our lives, choosing the safety of silence over the strength of personal integrity. In Hannah's story, we see God move this influential woman toward finding her own voice. Like Hannah, we can rediscover our voices by first naming who we are most truly and then daring to speak our unique messages of good news into the world.

To Consider . . .

Complex in design as we are, there is generally much more going on within our minds and hearts than we consciously recognize. For many of us, in times of stillness we can hear a stream of thoughts just below the surface. Take a few moments to be still. Then simply write what comes to mind, seeking to be open to whatever is going on inside you right now.

WHAT adult does not have painful stories from junior high or middle school in his or her memory bank? For me, the worst day came near the beginning of my eighth grade year.

Seventh grade had been rough: a new, larger school; shuffling from class to class all day long; dressing out in black stretchy shorts and a stiff white blouse for gym. All these strange dynamics were huge challenges to a shy, bookish, adolescent girl/woman, but they were nothing compared to the difficulty of finding a place of belonging among young teenage females.

The social strata seas for girls at Woodlawn Junior High were wild and woolly. This was the South in every exclusive sense of the word, and these girls were well trained. Growing up as the daughter of two "Yankees" and without any sisters, I wanted to be a part of a group of females more than anything. I desperately wanted someone to train me, instruct me, and affirm my place in the larger world of women.

In time, I found a good friend, Margaret. We quickly became life preservers for one another, saved repeatedly from the shifting seas of gossip, giggles, and ridicule that routinely drown other less fortunate souls. Not exactly what I had in mind, but at least I felt safe.

Tragically, sometime during the summer between my seventh and eighth grade years, a group of unthinking bureaucrats who had no idea what they were doing to my life redrew school district lines. You guessed it: My friend no longer attended my school. Once again, I was tossed into the sea alone and unprotected.

On the last day of the first week of eighth grade, I boldly entered the cafeteria with a strategy in mind. I headed for the sixth row of tables—long, peach-colored, pebbly Formica tables—noticing how sunlight from the window in front of me bathed my targeted spot. No one was sitting there yet, but I knew who would be. With uncharacteristic boldness I took a seat.

The first one out of the cafeteria line was Charlotte, the captain of this social ship. As a naïve fourteen-year-old girl, there were not many social moments I could read clearly, but this was one of the few. Even before she got to the table, I knew I was in trouble. Though I cannot recall what she said, I will never forget the look of contempt and superiority radiating from her face. The messages were clear: *Who are you that you would dare try to be included with us? Who are you to think you have anything to offer us? You have nothing to offer. You are not included. Go away.*

Quickly and ever so quietly, I moved to a table near the door, in the shadows facing the wall. I finished my lunch alone and in silence, full of shame for even daring to want to be part of a group of females.

Fast forward to age forty. In graduate school, a professor invited me to speak to our class about some of my personal insights into the story of Ruth. He allowed me to determine the extent of my contribution and how long I would speak. I prepared well, excited about the opportunity. Yet when the moment to speak arrived, I simply remained in my chair and offered only a few sentences to my classmates.

Curious about my own choice, I began to wonder what was going on inside me to sabotage and shortcut my voice. It did not take long to uncover the stifling echo: *Who are you to think you have anything to offer us?* For more than twenty years, the originating story of shame remained buried in my mind as the concluding message played on just below the surface. The pain of that eighth grade moment, experienced with magnified intensity in adolescence, began a long season of silence for me. Not silence in the literal sense of not speaking words but in the sense of carefully hiding the most creative, tender, and feminine parts of my soul. I denied voice to the truest parts of who I am.

As I continue to grow, I find that rediscovering and recovering my voice is one of the greatest challenges I face. Choosing to give up my silence has been a difficult call to repentance for me. Yet there has been help along the way. In recent years as I've begun to reexamine these early stories of my life and the long-held messages connected with them, I have discovered that many women, including ancient women, have been silenced in similar ways.

AN ANCIENT WOMAN'S SOUL

At different points of need in my life, the stories of women in Scripture have come to me like newfound, timely met friends. Hannah is one such friend. Her story in 1 Samuel 1–2 offered me wisdom about how to discover my voice at a time when I was first beginning to recognize and grapple with my silence. Her life offers us insight into uniquely feminine patterns of repentance and growth.

Hannah lived in a time of transition for the nation of Israel. Her son Samuel was the first prophet to anoint a king. As do most stories of new birth, this one begins with a woman in pain.

The Pain of Infertility

> *There was a certain man from Ramathaim, a Zuphite from the hill country of Ephraim, whose name was Elkanah son of Jeroham, the son of Elihu, the son of Tohu, the son of Zuph, an Ephraimite. He had two wives; one was called Hannah and the other Peninnah. Peninnah had children, but Hannah had none. (1:1-2)*

Though the description was simple—"Hannah had none"—the implications were not. Hannah lived those words out socially, religiously, and deeply personally. In Jewish culture, infertility was viewed as a curse. With no understanding of biology, it was always seen as the woman's fault and limitation. Though women were generally devalued by society, infertility diminished social status even further.

Religiously, the absence of children was interpreted as personal punishment for sin. As if that shame were not enough, being childless meant that a woman had no place in the ongoing work of God. The Jews understood their primary task to be that of growing a holy people, a nation set apart for God. A woman's part in that larger story of life was to bear children. If there were no children, she had no part.

The more internally personal implications seem obvious: a deeply experienced inadequacy, a feeling of being overlooked by God, a life-defining mantle of shame. Great, great pain. All these internal dynamics would naturally drive a woman deeper and deeper into hiding. I imagine Hannah walking through her days trying to be as inconspicuous as possible. The idea of living out the glory of her feminine soul, living a life of grace, beauty, and personal dignity, must have seemed unimaginable to her.

Unwise Love and Raging Jealousy

Year after year this man [Elkanah] went up from his town to worship and sacrifice to the Lord Almighty at Shiloh, where Hophni and Phinehas, the two sons of Eli, were priests of the Lord. Whenever the day came for Elkanah to sacrifice, he would give portions of the meat to his wife Peninnah and to all her sons and daughters. But to Hannah he gave a double portion because he loved her, and the Lord had closed her womb. And because the Lord had closed her womb, her rival kept provoking her in order to irritate her. This went on year after year. Whenever Hannah went up to the house of the Lord, her rival provoked her till she wept and would not eat. (verses 3-7)

Hannah was unusually fortunate in her day—her husband loved her in spite of her infertility. As a devout Jew, he sought to communicate that love to her in a concrete way: greater portions for sacrifice. Yet in the midst of his good intentions, it appears as if Elkanah's unwise choice of expression may have caused Hannah more pain. The favoritism meant to bless Hannah seems to have enraged her fellow wife, Peninnah, the one on the "less loved" end of that tipped scale. Year after year, not to mention infertile month after infertile month, Hannah's shame was before her. Verbal abuse and public ridicule multiplied the pain of her barrenness. No wonder she would not eat.

It is important to note that weeping and not eating are the only recorded responses we have of her—no words, no movement, no initiative of any kind in relationship with others. Her great pain seems to have silenced and paralyzed her. Like many women in similar circumstances, she shut down and turned inward.

Subtle Shaming

Elkanah her husband would say to her, "Hannah, why are you weeping? Why don't you eat? Why are you downhearted? Don't I mean more to you than ten sons?" (verse 8)

It is hard to imagine that Elkanah did not know why she was weeping, refusing to eat, and feeling downhearted. He saw her pain, undoubtedly felt it alongside her. He was not really seeking information about the state of her soul. So what was he trying to say?

Imagine for a moment what it must have felt like to be on the receiving end of these words. The logic seems sane, the reasoning sound: "Why keep torturing yourself wanting something you can never have? Why not simply decide to be content with what you do have?" Hard reasoning to counter, especially in a moment of conversation with a man who loves you and wants your pain (and his) to stop.

Look again at Elkanah's questions. What else was communicated? Hannah's well-meaning husband was seeking to diminish or dismiss Hannah's pain by putting it on a scale of his own creation: weighing her desire for a child against the goodness of his love for her. He subtly shamed her deeply held desire for a child even as he sought to elevate the power of his love in her life. He assumed his masculine perspective could resolve her feminine soul's anguish. He did not understand that hearts and desires have little regard for logic or for scales.

How could Hannah possibly respond? Should she deny her pain and desire? Or tell him his love was not enough? In his lack of wisdom, Elkanah once again accomplished the opposite of what he intended. Rather than offering true comfort to his wife, his subtle shaming let her know that her pain was no longer welcome in her relationship with him.

Subtly shaming messages like this one are a part of all of our lives. Consider the overweight woman whose friends grow weary of her pain and struggle to remain on a diet and say to her, "Oh, honey, why bother? We like you chunky, and no one else matters, right?" Or the daughter who is thrilled to find a pair of fancy pink sandals just right for the prom whose mother says, "Oh, no, dear, you don't want those. You already have those other beautiful shoes at home, remember?" Or the woman who chooses to go back to work whose husband says, "Isn't what I provide enough? I'd *kill* to not have to go to work every day." All are seemingly supportive messages that subtly shame a vulnerably expressed desire.

As women, we are often uniquely susceptible to this kind of less than noble persuasion. We too easily doubt the goodness of our feminine desires, especially in the face of seeming support and convincing logic, simply because our desires are connected so deeply with our hearts and emotions. The fact that these painful dynamics are written within these ancient stories can be very healing. God knows our pain and cares about the ways we hurt and struggle.

Silenced from Within

Once when they had finished eating and drinking in Shiloh, Hannah stood up. (verse 9)

Again, we are not told of any verbal response from Hannah. A clearer translation is found in the nasb: "Then Hannah rose after eating and drinking in Shiloh." The language of verse 9 indicates that Hannah was finally eating and drinking again with her family or community. With that choice, she began to actively silence, even "stuff," her grief and pain. She began to pretend. Or maybe she had unthinkingly chosen in this moment to "go along to get along." Let's face it. Shame usually works, at least for a while.

Just as no one else can stop our physical expression of voice, short of killing us, the same is also true of voice in the larger sense. Hannah *chose* silence. She had become silenced from within. Maybe all those messages she had heard and replayed from her long season of infertility now echoed in her head, reinforcing the words of Elkanah. For whatever reason, she opted for silence and elected pretense: She began to eat and drink. Hannah began to hide the truest parts of her feminine soul.

It is critical that we own the choosing of our silence so we can recognize that we have the power to choose differently. The fact that we opt for silence in times of pain or perhaps for the sake of sheer survival, physical or emotional, does not mean we are forever destined to that choice. Hannah chose silence. But not for long.

From somewhere deep inside her soul, grace met her, and she stood up. Hannah's first act of initiative is a very powerful nonverbal clue for us as readers. Transformation was happening. In the midst of unspeakable pain, Hannah's voice was born.

Many of us have grown up in the church with a rather linear idea of the spiritual growth process, often taken from 2 Timothy 3:16-17: "All Scripture is God-breathed and is useful for teaching, rebuking, correcting and training in righteousness, so that the man of God may be thoroughly equipped for every good work." Teaching, rebuking, correcting, and training. These ideas and patterns are notably absent in this ancient woman's story. Hannah's change in life direction seems instead like a natural birthing process. We have certainly noted the presence of pain. As her story unfolds, observe the gradual birthing of this transformed feminine soul.

Expressing Heartfelt Desire

> *Now Eli the priest was sitting on a chair by the doorpost of the Lord's temple. In bitterness of soul Hannah wept much and prayed to the Lord. And she made a vow, saying, "O Lord Almighty, if you will only look upon your servant's misery and remember me, and not forget your servant but give her a son, then I will give him to the Lord for all the days of his life, and no razor will ever be used on his head." (verses 9-11)*

In her first recorded act after standing up, Hannah sought the presence of God. With nothing else to bring, she went to the temple accompanied only by her pain and unquenchable desire for a child. Note her wise and honest self-awareness. She felt utterly empty, forgotten, and probably invisible to the One she sought. My guess is that she *thought* little and *felt* intensely as she prayed.

Perhaps Hannah realized for the first time that a child was not the greatest object of her desire. In her prayer, even as she asked for a child, she surrendered the same. Her words seem to reflect a new and rare wisdom: What she wanted most of all was to be seen and not forgotten by God. Such vulnerable desires as these speak to the core of our feminine souls. Though the child was important, he was *more* importantly a sign, a tangible symbol, of God's love for her.

Learning to Speak

As she kept on praying to the Lord, Eli observed her mouth. Hannah was praying in her heart, and her lips were moving but her voice was not heard. Eli thought she was drunk and said to her, "How long will you keep on getting drunk? Get rid of your wine." (verses 12-14)

First she stood; next she moved her lips without a sound. Could the process of coming to voice be illustrated any more incrementally for us? When we begin to move away from the comfortable prison of our silence, the process of discovering our voice will not be smooth or swift. Like any new endeavor, it will take time to become clear about who we are, what we think and feel, and what we have to say.

This learning process will no doubt be disturbing to others. Any shift in relationships and roles is disruptive to familiar patterns. Though we may hesitate to admit it, some in our lives will not *want* to hear us, know us, or understand us. That is especially true when, like Hannah's, our first words reveal pain, anger, or grief. As with Hannah, miscommunication will happen and accusations will fly.

"I Am Not"/"I Am"

"Not so, my lord," Hannah replied, "I am a woman who is deeply troubled. I have not been drinking wine or beer; I was pouring out my soul to the Lord. Do not take your servant for a

wicked woman; I have been praying here out of my great anguish and grief." (verses 15-16)

Notice how Hannah responded to this challenge. Just as "no" is one of the first words spoken by a child, so also a woman's journey toward voice often begins as she speaks out against an injustice.

Hannah's words were a dance of "I am not" and "I am" statements. As she began to speak, her words were primarily descriptive in nature. For the first time, we see her refuting rather than receiving and internalizing the messages others were giving her. Just as her silencing came first from the outside and then was internalized by her, so now that process began to reverse. She had to learn who she was internally before she could offer her voice to others. For Hannah, a significant part of naming herself was unapologetically claiming her feminine soul's unmet desire.

Her process of growth toward God was connected to a larger sense of self and voice, not a diminishing of self. Like the other women we will meet throughout this book, Hannah was being called by God away from smallness and hiding toward a fuller sense of her feminine soul. It is absolutely revolutionary that this Jewish woman's first "no" was said to a priest. Such an observation becomes even more important as we witness all these generations later the role of heroine that Hannah has assumed in both the Jewish and Christian traditions.

Hannah's story models the fact that at some point in our growth process, most of us will be called to confront false messages we have received from religious authorities in our lives. Hannah mentors us in that most painful of moments, giving us permission to engage a critical and difficult developmental task.

Going Her Way

Eli answered, "Go in peace, and may the God of Israel grant you what you have asked of him."
She said, "May your servant find favor in your eyes." Then she went her way and ate something, and her face was no longer downcast.

Early the next morning they arose and worshiped before the Lord and then went back to their home at Ramah. Elkanah lay with Hannah his wife, and the Lord remembered her. So in the course of time Hannah conceived and gave birth to a son. She named him Samuel [sounds like the Hebrew word for "heard of God"], saying, "Because I asked the Lord for him."

When the man Elkanah went up with all his family to offer the annual sacrifice to the Lord and to fulfill his vow, Hannah did not go. She said to her husband, "After the boy is weaned, I will take him and present him before the Lord, and he will live there always."

"Do what seems best to you," Elkanah her husband told her. "Stay here until you have weaned him; only may the Lord make good his word." So the woman stayed at home and nursed her son until she had weaned him. (verses 17-23)

Did you notice Hannah's energy and initiative compared to the opening scenes in her story? Even before she became pregnant, we see a changed woman. In fact, the way the story of the pregnancy is told, it almost feels incidental. We see that *Hannah* asked for her son, *Hannah* named him, *Hannah* chose not to go on the annual family temple venture. Her self-awareness gave birth to a personal vision and sense of calling. The internal voice of her restored feminine soul now guided her life. These first expressions of this voice were within her family, but soon her voice began to be heard in her larger spiritual community.

Taking Her Place in the Kingdom

After he was weaned, she took the boy with her, young as he was, along with a three-year-old bull, an ephah of flour and a skin of wine, and brought him to the house of the Lord at Shiloh. When they had slaughtered the bull, they brought the boy to Eli, and she said to him, "As surely as you live, my lord, I am the woman who stood here beside you praying to the Lord. I prayed for this

*child, and the Lord has granted me what I asked of him. So now
I give him to the Lord. For his whole life he will be given over to
the Lord." And he worshiped the Lord there. (verses 24-28)*

Grace lived on as Hannah's voice grew stronger. No longer feeling
forgotten by God, she had a new sense of personhood that she brought
into her relationship with her Healer. Recall that as her story began, she
offered the sacrifices Elkanah gave her to offer. Here she brought to God
her own gifts: a bull, flour, wine, and her son. As she spoke with Eli, she
said, "I am . . . I prayed . . . I asked . . . I give." Such "I's" are not
unbridled sinful selfishness as we are sometimes taught; rather, they
express a healthy sense of self. No longer hiding in the safety of
invisibility, Hannah's newfound feminine soul and self allowed her to
offer *herself* in relationship to God even as she brought her gifts.

Proclaiming Her Good News

It is difficult for me to imagine all that Hannah must have been feeling as
she brought her ever-so-young son that day for the purpose of leaving
him. Yet in her song of worship, we begin to glimpse an amazing
intimate knowledge of and confidence in God that I am sure must have
carried her through the excruciating moment:

Then Hannah prayed and said:

*"My heart rejoices in the Lord;
    in the Lord my horn is lifted high.
My mouth boasts over my enemies,
    for I delight in your deliverance.*

*"There is no one holy like the Lord;
    there is no one besides you;
    there is no Rock like our God.*

"Do not keep talking so proudly

23

or let your mouth speak such arrogance,
for the Lord is a God who knows,
*   and by him deeds are weighed.*

"The bows of the warriors are broken,
*   but those who stumbled are armed with strength.*
Those who were full hire themselves out for food,
*   but those who were hungry hunger no more.*
She who was barren has borne seven children,
*   but she who has had many sons pines away.*

"The Lord brings death and makes alive;
*   he brings down to the grave and raises up.*
The Lord sends poverty and wealth;
*   he humbles and he exalts.*
He raises the poor from the dust
*   and lifts the needy from the ash heap;*
he seats them with princes
*   and has them inherit a throne of honor.*

"For the foundations of the earth are the Lord's;
*   upon them he has set the world.*
He will guard the feet of his saints,
*   but the wicked will be silenced in darkness.*

"It is not by strength that one prevails;
*   those who oppose the Lord will be shattered.*
He will thunder against them from heaven;
*   the Lord will judge the ends of the earth.*

"He will give strength to his king
*   and exalt the horn of his anointed." (2:1-10)*

Hannah knew that God saw her, remembered her, and acted on her behalf. She also knew that God would do the same for her young son. Her story of enormous pain became her song of praise. This was her personal proclamation of good news, her unique gospel message that she offered boldly to the world.

Interestingly, Hannah's song formed the basis of Mary's song, the Magnificat, recorded in Luke 2. Because Hannah abandoned her silence and discovered her voice, her beautiful testimony sang on through the mother of Jesus Himself and continues to do so through both Jews and Christians today. What a voice!

Hannah models for us a powerful feminine growth paradigm. Her transformation has a different rhythm to it than the rebuke, conviction, repentance, and transformation pattern so often offered in our churches. Though clearly Hannah repented in the sense of changing how she lived her life, it did not look at all like what most of us call repentance. Again, this feminine soul dynamic is a backward, upside-down, in-a-mirror kind of pattern when compared to the other.

As I began to spend time with Hannah during that particular season of my life in my early forties, I slowly became willing to abandon my comfortable prison of silence. Because I had received so many false messages about myself over the years, especially with regard to my femininity, it took years to simply discover my true story of "I am not/I am." Part of what I discovered is that I love being a woman and being with women. My first expressions of those passions were wordless choices such as curled hair, softer colors, and long lunches. As I have lived further into and out of my voice, I have begun to speak and write, proclaiming my own personal story of good news. The fact that God has provided a way for this book to be published is sweet and miraculous redemption indeed!

Hannah has been my faithful companion and mentor on this long, rough, and grace-filled journey of repentance. I join my voice with hers, daring to offer you the good news that God longs to hear the voice of *your* feminine soul. How will you respond to such a winsome invitation to speak?

YOUR JOURNEY

For personal reflection and group discussion

1. We all have experienced infertility in one form or another. There are areas in our lives of unfulfilled desires and long-held, deeply rooted dreams never realized. God seems to have forgotten us. Some of our struggles may be obvious like Hannah's; others we keep well hidden, at times hesitating to acknowledge the depth of these longings even to ourselves. Name some of your points of "infertility."

2. From time to time, most of us experience the delight of finding people in our lives with whom we feel especially comfortable. These are the folks in whose presence we can be completely and unapologetically ourselves: opinionated, passionate, creative, free—the good, the bad, and the ugly. Describe one such relationship from your past or present.

3. There are also relational experiences that have the opposite effect on us. There are people with whom we tend to shut down, either consciously or unconsciously, sometimes understanding why we do it and other times not understanding it at all. Describe such an experience.

4. As we look back on our own stories, we are often reluctant to acknowledge the very real pain and harm that have come into our lives through well-intentioned but unwise people. Describe an example of painfully unwise love from your own experiences.

5. The relational dynamics of subtle shaming are difficult, if not impossible, to see in a moment of relationship. Yet often they are felt and can be discerned later, sometimes experienced as a sense of walking away from people who love you, feeling hurt and unsure of how the injury happened. Again, these are difficult to acknowledge because often the other person's desire is to end your pain (and theirs) or to save you from a grief God may be calling you (and those

who love you) to live. Can you recall a time when some well-meaning person in your life sought to diminish your desires or pain and ended up shaming you into "contentment"? Describe one such incident.

6. None of us is a complete stranger to intentional abuse. The old saying "Sticks and stones may break my bones, but words will never hurt me" is an outright lie! Those incidents of public ridicule that are connected to deeply held dreams are often our most painful moments. Write down one such story from your past. How did you respond?

7. As in my story from junior high, these shaming events leave lasting messages in our minds. What messages did you internalize from your stories of pain? What voices inside you have encouraged you to silence your own desires, to "go along to get along"?

8. Describe a moment of grace in your life when deep pain gave birth to a new way of being. When have you "stood up"?

9. Think back to your areas of infertility. Might you have desires for God that run even deeper than the desires most immediately in your awareness? What does the fulfillment of your immediate desire symbolize for you in your relationship with God?

10. Make your own "I am not/I am" lists. Be especially mindful of past "error" messages you have internalized that you can now refute.

11. As Christian women, we often struggle with misunderstandings about God's view of the concept of self. How do you generally feel as you relate to God? Do you feel distant? Small? Fully present as yourself? Hidden? Less than human? Invisible? Dirty? Like an actress? Something else? Will you dare to believe that God wants to relate to you as a person with a healthy, beautiful, and strong sense of your feminine soul?

12. What is your good news? How do you or will you proclaim it?

CHAPTER TWO

Giving Up Games, Daring to Be Honest

THE WOMAN AT THE WELL IN JOHN 4

As women, we often play relational games with both God and ourselves, refusing to be honest about what we want most in life. We use our astute relational sensitivity and creativity against ourselves, spending our lives looking for water that simply will not satisfy. Layer by layer, Jesus drew the woman at the well toward repentance, peeling away her self-frustrating defenses. As she dared to be honest, He touched the core of her feminine soul.

To Consider . . .

What do you expect from God in terms of relationship? What do you want? Polite acceptance? Help with the ordinary things of life? Intimacy? Passion?

"IT'S absolutely devastating."

As Susan spoke, I strained to imagine her experience. Her sentences were brief, interrupted often by pauses to catch her breath. Struggling even with supplemental oxygen, she continued.

"The fear is unreal. Do you know the odds of a successful transplant?"

I did know the odds. The odds were not good.

As a chaplain in the hospital Susan frequently used, I had journeyed with Susan for four years. During those years, her condition had steadily declined. She had many close calls with death, narrowly escaping each time, becoming more fragile with each battle. Every time I saw her, it seemed she was facing a new and different challenge.

When I first met Susan, her greatest desire was to live as normally as possible, though she had consented to the fact that she would need help. Her challenge was finding affordable, reliable assistance. A former insurance agent, Susan was a capable administrator and self-advocate. She soon had met the challenge and was on her way home with great plans. Through our conversations, I heard the details of her efforts.

As her condition worsened and normalcy was no longer possible even with great assistance from others, Susan's focus of desire changed to simply being able to walk across a room without becoming breathless. Her only hope was a transplant, and Susan took on this even larger challenge. For three years she put all of her energy into one vision of hope, a single acceptable option. For three years she worked hard for insurance approval. Again, she gathered support and organized fundraisers to cover ancillary expenses. Whether in or out of the hospital, she worked with great intensity toward her goal. Her drive and spirit were amazing. When we spoke, I heard her plans.

Susan filled those three years so full of the pressing challenge of the transplant that it was easy to avoid an awareness of her own current suffering, much less the deeper questions of her soul. There was no talk of anything but a successful transplant. Having listened carefully to Susan for several years, it seemed to me that perhaps she was playing a game with life, seeking to protect the most tender and frightened parts of her feminine soul by simply not acknowledging them. Something within her could not yet dare complete honesty. She was not sure there was a hope beyond the physical healing she was counting on, so she lived as best she could within the boundaries of the only hope she knew.

The transplant did not come, and Susan's condition continued to deteriorate. Sometimes God does not cooperate with our strategies or even our deepest desires. Instead, our Healer draws us toward a reality we would rather not face. God woos us beyond the confines of hope as we know it, inviting us to grow in ways we are not at all sure we are ready for.

That day as I walked into her room, it was clear that for the first time, Susan's method for making her life work was not working. Another layer of challenge, a deeper desire than breath itself, a more certain hope than physical healing was beginning to surface. Ready or not, Susan dared honesty. I heard no more details about all her efforts and plans. That day our conversation was very different.

As she began to speak about the risk of a transplant, Susan acknowledged the very real possibility of her death. Finding the courage to face another level of challenge, Susan expressed her deep desire for peace with God. That day, for the first time, she brought her whole self to our conversation—no games, nothing hidden. We spoke openly of suffering, fear, and death, as well as comfort, peace, and God. With layers of games peeled away and hearts open and honestly vulnerable, God brought deep and eternal healing and hope.

Reflecting on our conversation later, I realized that I, too, struggle with this multilevel dance of challenges and hidden desires, bringing only parts of myself into relationships with others. I, too, am pretty successful at playing games as I try to keep my heart safe—a success that sometimes costs me dearly.

For example, I recently returned from an extended personal retreat. Meeting daily with my spiritual director, we made good progress weeding through issues of discernment regarding a pending job change. The day before I left, I mentioned my marital struggles—almost in passing. Addressing issues of my "hands" (the "doing" things in my life) was far easier than confronting issues of the heart—relationships and desires that strike to the core of my being. A wise woman, my director caught the clue, following that path and eventually noting my avoidance. Sadly, my retreat was nearly over by then. Though I had certainly not wasted the time, I was grieved that my game had worked so well, that I had not availed myself of this kind woman's comfort and insight.

Like my friend Susan, I spend much of my time caught in a maze of lesser challenges, layers of self-frustrating games. At times, I refuse to be honest, even with myself, especially when I am about to come face-to-face with hurt or pain or loss that I would rather avoid. In those moments, I find myself glossing over my heart's desires and escaping into a superficial awareness of what is going on inside me. My games show up in odd ways at the strangest moments. I might avoid the pain of recognizing how little I know of my college-age children's expanding lives by concentrating on making the perfect meal when they are home for the weekend rather than taking the time to really engage and listen. I might avoid dealing with my anger toward my husband by organizing a girls' night out. I have even been guilty of avoiding God by planning a Sunday school lesson instead of spending much-needed time alone.

In those times of self-avoidance and self-frustration, even when I get what I thought I wanted most, I remain unsatisfied. I spin and spin as I try to manage my time and fix my life, to finally "get my act together." The urgent matters demand my consideration; the deeper ones remain unnoticed. In those moments, the voices of others draw my attention more than the cries of my own soul. When my games "succeed," the truest parts of my feminine soul remain hidden—even from me.

Thankfully, in my struggle to live more honestly, freer of my own games, I find that I am not alone. I not only am companioned by struggling women such as Susan, but I also have another very old friend.

AN ANCIENT WOMAN'S SOUL

The story of the woman at the well in John 4 has intrigued me for years. She's an old friend of mine whose wisdom I seek from time to time. She, too, struggled to understand the greater challenges of her life. She, too, struggled to know herself and live honestly. Like me, she often played games, seeking to protect herself. I see her encounter with Jesus as a gentle unfolding, layer by layer, of her deepest challenges and hidden desires. His ever-welcoming, ever-deepening invitations wooed her toward honesty and a uniquely feminine kind of repentance.

A Daring Invitation

When a Samaritan woman came to draw water, Jesus said to her, "Will you give me a drink?" (His disciples had gone into the town to buy food.)

The Samaritan woman said to him, "You are a Jew and I am a Samaritan woman. How can you ask me for a drink?"

(For Jews do not associate with Samaritans.) (verses 7-9)

Jesus initiated the conversation. Knowing one of the easiest ways to engage a woman, He simply asked for help.

The woman replied sharply, evidencing the ache of one of her daily challenges: social stigma. As a Samaritan woman, she was accustomed to contempt from Jews. Considering that she was drawing water at noon rather than during the cool of the day, she was probably avoiding social contact, possibly due to additional rejection from her own people. She knew all the right social moves to protect her feminine soul from harm.

It appears she was somewhat surprised that Jesus even spoke to her at all. Accustomed to being invisible, she was astonished He even considered her worthy to serve Him. I hear pain and a deep sense of despair reflected in her cynical "support" of the status quo policy of social separation. It was a game she played to keep her heart from admitting how much she wanted life to be different. Ironically, she questioned the very One who was inviting her in this moment to be seen and respected as a woman, free from social stigma.

A Deeper Dare

Jesus answered her, "If you knew the gift of God and who it is that asks you for a drink, you would have asked him and he would have given you living water." (verse 10)

Rather than backing away from her cynical response, as we often fear He will, Jesus moved a step closer. His response did not dismiss her pain but transcended it. He dared her not only to believe in the reality of this present moment of experienced dignity and acceptance but also to begin to want even more from Him.

Jesus questioned her inability to see good gifts, available help, from God. Jesus knew this was a huge challenge for her. He was aware of a core struggle in most women: receiving the care of others. He began to invite her to become deeply aware of her thirst, more honest about what she wanted most in life. Jesus spoke to a longing far from her consciousness, long ago banished to the realm of the impossible.

Running from Honesty

"Sir," the woman said, "you have nothing to draw with and the well is deep. Where can you get this living water? Are you greater than our father Jacob, who gave us the well and drank from it himself, as did also his sons and his flocks and herds?"

Jesus answered, "Everyone who drinks this water will be thirsty again, but whoever drinks the water I give him will never thirst. Indeed, the water I give him will become in him a spring of water welling up to eternal life." (verses 11-14)

As Jesus invited this oft-rejected woman to a reborn awareness of her thirst, she understood His invitation enough to see it as dangerous. My guess is that her life had been a long string of disappointed hopes and unfulfilled desires. Perhaps she had sworn never to want anything from anyone or to let herself hope again. So she ran hard and fast. She offered her own challenge, her dare that attempted to dismiss Jesus Himself as well as the possibility of goodness.

Undaunted by her defense, Jesus deepened the challenge as He sweetened the invitation. He invited her to believe in goodness *and* abundance, personally and freely given. Notice the incremental invitations Jesus offered this woman as He wooed her with goodness and kindness. Contrast that with Paul's dramatic conversion on the road to Damascus with bright lights and blindness (see Acts 9:1-19) or Jesus' conversation with Nicodemus in the previous chapter of this same gospel (John 3). As a man with a lot of religious clout in that day, Nicodemus came to Jesus at night, risking a lot, seeking some answers from this controversial and intriguing Rabbi. Jesus left him with more confusion than clarity, more insults than affirmations. There is a drivenness to many examples of transformation in men that contrasts with the drawing nature of this gentle, more incremental approach.

Daring to Believe

The woman said to him, "Sir, give me this water so that I won't get thirsty and have to keep coming here to draw water." (verse 15)

Suddenly, we sense a shift within this woman. Jesus' persistence had piqued her curiosity. Cautiously, she dared both openness and honesty. Her first step toward repentance came in the form of letting her simple physical desire begin to surface. All she thought she wanted was fresh water to drink, an artesian well, a break from her burdensome daily chores. Though ready to receive pragmatic help, she could not yet acknowledge her feminine soul's desire for more.

In her limited wisdom, it seems she offered Jesus a prescription for how she wanted God to love her. Maybe she wanted Him to play her game. It might be that she needed to stay in control for a bit longer. Her prescription sounds a bit like a demand.

Exposing a Deeper Longing

He told her, "Go, call your husband and come back."

"I have no husband," she replied.

Jesus said to her, "You are right when you say you have no husband. The fact is, you have had five husbands, and the man

34

you now have is not your husband. What you have just said is quite true." (verses 16-18)

Though the woman's first step toward faith was still within her "game," Jesus knew that this first step toward receiving relationship was huge. Her feminine soul was moving toward repentance, choosing to live differently. He also knew that she was asking for far too little, yet He did not rebuke her in any way. Jesus moved toward helping her become more honest about her own deeper longings. As before, He did not dismiss her request. He transcended it. Knowing that self-awareness is far from automatic and that often the relationship we run from with the greatest intensity is our relationship with ourselves, He incrementally challenged her, seeking to help her know her own heart.

This woman at the well thought what she wanted most of all was help with the ordinary burdens of life. Jesus knew that her life held a much deeper desire: intimacy. So He exposed the next layer. The woman replied honestly, vulnerably. Jesus affirmed her honesty.

We do not know the history of why she had had five husbands and why the one she was living with at the time was not her husband. Perhaps she had been widowed five times and simply could not stand the loss of another husband. Most assume, however, that she was a woman of ill repute (possibly evidenced by the fact that she was drawing water at noon). Could it be that her unrecognized and unacknowledged desire for intimacy left her seeking from men a kind of intimacy that would never satisfy? Jesus invited her to give up games and dare to experience a new, more satisfying relationship.

It is critical to note that Jesus was not seeking to increase her shame but to strip away the layers of games. He sought to reveal the depth of the thirst of her feminine soul that was unable to be quenched by anyone or anything other than God. He wanted her to own a thirst far more real and painful than the thirst of her body that had brought her to this well.

A Mistaken Assumption

"Sir," the woman said, "I can see that you are a prophet. Our fathers worshiped on this mountain, but you Jews claim that the place where we must worship is in Jerusalem." (verses 19-20)

A discerning woman, the woman at the well recognized the presence of the Holy. Yet she also seems to have mistakenly assumed that the primary way to relationship with the Holy was compliance to some elusive standard of "right." She made a first step, a move toward God, but it was one that feels a bit like a stiff-arm. Maybe she found a way that seemed safer. It was easier to engage her ability to do good than to risk the possibility of being loved. Rather than acknowledging her deep desire for relationship, she appears to have spoken only of her desire to be right.

For many women, the practice of duty and servitude is far easier than daring to believe in genuine intimate relationship. How often we spend hours and hours learning about God even as we avoid being still enough to meet Him face-to-face. We find time for service projects but not for personal devotional time. We rattle off our list of prayer petitions without pausing to listen to the cry of our own souls or to receive the comfort of the Holy Spirit. As Jesus stands before us, seeking to love us, we ask Him which church we should visit next Sunday or what book we should read next.

The Ultimate Invitation

Jesus declared, "Believe me, woman, a time is coming when you will worship the Father neither on this mountain nor in Jerusalem. You Samaritans worship what you do not know; we worship what we do know, for salvation is from the Jews. Yet a time is coming and has now come when the true worshipers will worship the Father in spirit and truth, for they are the kind of worshipers the Father seeks. God is spirit, and his worshipers must worship in spirit and in truth." (verses 21-24)

Once again, Jesus did not rebuke or correct this good woman but continued to gently challenge and draw her to a truer knowledge of herself and the Holy. Jesus shifted the conversation from a focus on distant standards to the revelation that the Holy desires relationship, true and spiritual relationship. Indeed, the Holy seeks it.

Stepping Toward Honesty

The woman said, "I know that Messiah" (called Christ) "is coming.
When he comes, he will explain everything to us." (verse 25)

She caught the shift. And took another step. She now expected relationship, even relationship with an individual—the Messiah. She might have even felt her own desire for such. Still, she could imagine it only as a distant possibility, not a present reality. She could not yet see the Holy's pursuit of her in this moment—His invitation to leave the games, the cloaked safety of the invisibly anonymous "us," for a sense of her own personal desire for relationship with God.

Connecting with the Holy

Then Jesus declared, "I who speak to you am he." (verse 26)

Read those simple words again—slowly. Do you sense the crescendo of this conversation? The Holy claimed a new name: the One who speaks to you, the woman at the well. The Holy was present, available, touchable, seeking relationship now, just as He began the conversation by asking for a drink of water. God was not distant and remote, but intimate and seeking. God was not abandoning her as so many who had gone before, but affirming her with His very presence. God was not content with her distance, her hiding, or her games, but invited her into an honest, living relationship, then and there.

Forever Changed

Then, leaving her water jar, the woman went back to the town and said to the people, "Come, see a man who told me everything I ever did. Could this be the Christ?" . . .

Many of the Samaritans from that town believed in him because of the woman's testimony, "He told me everything I ever did." (verses 28-29,39)

Though we do not read a direct reply from this changed woman, we see beyond what any statement could communicate. We see her transformed life. The one so focused on the physical challenge of gathering water left her jar. This woman once caught up in the pain of social stigma now sought out her community. The one so bent on hiding behind her games was celebrating being fully known by the Holy. Her transformed feminine soul became an amazing source of transformation for many.

It is significant that this woman chose to celebrate being known so truly and completely by Jesus. There is within most feminine souls a deep, deep abiding desire to be fully known and completely loved. (Men certainly want this intimacy as well, but their God-ordained design leads them to seek respect and significance even more.) For this ancient woman who had probably experienced so much rejection and pain, Jesus' call to relationship addressed her greatest area of need for healing, hope, and transformation.

Repentance for this woman came not in the form of conviction, rebuke, or correction but in her willingness to be known by Jesus—another unique demonstration of what repentance can look like for a woman. It seems backward, upside down, and in a mirror in comparison to our more traditional ideas about how spiritual growth happens. Because this woman dared to believe she was known and loved by the Holy, abundant water welled up within her parched soul, deeply satisfying her entire being. Repentance happened; her way of being in the world radically changed.

This ancient woman's former challenges did not disappear. Social stigma and physical and emotional needs still existed. Yet having found the courage to honestly face her deepest desire for relationship with the

Holy, she now possessed an expectation of goodness and abundance, hopefulness and strength that tempered future challenges. Seeing her feminine soul through the affirming eyes of Jesus, she was transformed.

This woman-of-old's transformation reminds me of my friend Susan. Our conversation that day was difficult. Her honesty and courage amazed me. She spoke of death and of the things she wanted to accomplish before she died, conversations she longed to have, good-byes that needed to be said. She talked about things she would leave undone. No longer hiding the present behind the future, she began to *live* her last days on earth. Susan reclaimed her life, her present, her feminine soul that day. She no longer needed the games. Confident in the love of Christ for her just as she was, she found new hope as she faced life's greatest challenge: death. Though she continued to work toward a transplant until her death a few months later, she now worked out of the peace and strength that comes with living honestly rather than the avoidance and desperation of games.

Inspired by both Susan and the woman at the well, I, too, am seeking to live more honestly. More aware of my self-frustrating avoidance games, I seek to listen to myself more consciously, often through journaling or some form of reflective creativity. I've come to realize that self-awareness is a critical first step to honesty, the kind of honesty essential to hearing and connecting intimately with God. Though my discipline comes and goes as the lesser challenges scream around me, I am quicker to sense and respond to the need to reconnect with myself and the Holy One who sees and knows me so well.

I invite you now to join your story with ours, to hear the voice of the challenging Holy drawing you, peeling away your games and defenses. Jesus is inviting you to a new level of honesty where God can speak to the depths of your feminine soul. Will you dare to be known and loved?

YOUR JOURNEY

For personal reflection and group discussion

1. Make a list of three current challenges you are facing:

    *   One that is daily, urgent
    *   One that you sense is important but not urgent

- One on a soul, core, or existential level

2. Which level of challenge receives most of your energy and attention? If you were to talk with Jesus about your current challenges, what would you expect to hear?

3. What might "water"—good, satisfying, and abundant—look like for you today? Recall that Jesus does not shame lesser desires; He simply invites us to be aware of greater ones, also.

4. The woman at the well thought at first that all she wanted was an artesian well. Do you have a script for God's expressions of love toward you, perhaps even a demand? Is God cooperating with your game? If not, can you sense a challenge to become aware of a still deeper desire that you have not previously acknowledged?

5. Looking with His clear eyes at your life, what cycles of repeated dissatisfaction and self-frustrating games might Jesus see? As with the woman at the well, the exposure is not meant to shame you but to draw you toward life.

6. Do you ever opt for the less vulnerable life of "duty-driven" spirituality? What would an objective examination of your use of time regarding your relationship with God reveal?

7. Describe your first love, a romantic relational experience, or an intimate friendship. How does your relationship with God reflect the elements of that relationship?

8. When and where have you felt the Holy seeking intimate relationship with you? How will you dare this week to be still long enough to hear, "I who speak to you am he"?

CHAPTER THREE

Giving Up Busyness, Daring to be Still

MARTHA OF BETHANY IN LUKE 10:38-42

Though many of us long for rest, few find it. The world offers us many easy excuses for the frantic pace of our lives. We rarely recognize our choice to avoid stillness. We cannot quit running until we dare to face the question, "Whom or what am I running from?" In Martha's story, we observe that Jesus sees our busyness, understands what drives us as women, and invites us to self-awareness and self-care.

To Consider . . .

Imagine your life with half your available waking hours and all your present responsibilities. How would you adjust? What would you let go of? What would you hold on to?

MY friend Sharon is a very wise woman. She is also a very courageous woman. And, like all of us, sometimes she is a woman too busy for her own good.

I first met Sharon more than a decade ago when my children were school age and hers were in preschool. One of the things I admired most about her was the balance in her life. As the pastor's wife of a large church, that was no easy task. Even with the demands of young ones, she managed to make time for herself. A personal trainer by profession, she was a very disciplined woman. She exercised, ate right, and even took regular weekends away from her family for what she called "mommy time."

After I had enjoyed our friendship for the better part of five years, Sharon's husband took a new job in another state, and we lost touch for the next five. Last year, we were able to reconnect through mutual friends and enjoyed a long weekend together at the beach. Sharon recounted for me her intriguing soul journey since we had last visited.

With the move to a larger city and her children finally all in school, Sharon's career really took off. She found great satisfaction in working with clients, offering them help toward shaping healthier bodies, minds, and souls. As her children grew, they became involved outside the home in soccer, band, dance, and their church's youth program.

As the pace of her life picked up, so, too, did the intensity of her personal challenges. Her father, with whom she had always had a strained relationship, died suddenly. Within months of that loss, she also suffered the miscarriage of her fourth child. Her husband's new church was more consuming for him and at times an outright painful place for her to be. In the larger city, finances were also stressed even with her higher income.

"But I was *fine*," Sharon said with a soft chuckle. "You know what fine stands for, don't you? Frustrated. Insecure. Neurotic. Emotional."

My friend went on to tell me that her husband had given her a gift certificate for a weekend personal retreat at a monastery a few hours from their home. In fact, he had been there himself several times since gifting her with the weekend. "That envelope sat on my dresser for months," Sharon said. "You know me, when my kids were small, that retreat would have been scheduled within the hour! But I just couldn't find the time.

"But, boy, did I *need* to find the time! I felt as if all I did all day long was yell at the kids—shoving and moving them from here to there for all their activities. I was exhausted, and I was gaining weight to boot, even though I was exercising constantly. I went to the doctor, and he said I was healthy. Here I was, the professional on 'balance,' and I was a mess. Finally, I did it—I put it on my calendar and took that retreat."

Sharon recounted how after arriving at the center on a Friday afternoon, she went walking in the woods even before she unpacked her car. With twenty-seven acres of land at her disposal, she felt as if she had walked forever by the time she made it back to her vehicle. As she unloaded the dozen books and half-dozen CDs she had brought with her on her three-day retreat, she realized for the first time that she was afraid of being alone. So afraid, in fact, that she had brought all these additional "voices" with her on her "personal" retreat.

Entering her small room, she noted the simple, comfortable furnishings. The warm browns and beiges began to soothe her frazzled soul. The uncluttered space invited her to breathe in more deeply, to exhale more slowly. Exhausted from her walk and with the quiet seeping into her body, she climbed up on her bed and sat still, really still, for the first time in a very long time.

As she saw herself with newborn awareness, an image came to mind. She felt as if she had arrived at the monastery clothed in a stiff, burdensome, ugly, noisy suit of armor. Slowly, that armor began to melt off her body. Unexpectedly, she began to feel frightened. Her breathing quickened. She suddenly knew what she was deeply afraid of: There might not be anyone beneath the armor.

Thankfully, there was someone: a woman.

As I said, Sharon is a wise woman. So though she barely knew her true self at that moment, she somehow knew she liked her. She could tell that this woman, this tender feminine soul, needed her attention and nurturing. Sharon found the courage to acknowledge that she had been avoiding herself for a very long time.

My friend continued, "I used to know her—way back when. How did I lose her? Was it the sadness over Daddy's death? Or the baby? I never really had a chance to say good-bye to either one. Or things at church? Or just the busyness? Somehow, rather than really living my life, the good and the bad, I just kept stuffing it all inside and putting on a new piece of armor to keep it covered. I think the most effective piece of armor was the busyness itself. I knew that if I ever really stopped, I would just fall apart. And I did!"

Sharon described the remainder of the weekend as a blessedly healing time. The armor she had held on to for so long was safe but also restrictive. She was ready to finally let it go. Amazingly, even in a space of time as brief as a weekend, alone and still, Sharon got reacquainted with herself at a whole new level. Continuing to explore the image that had come so powerfully into her mind, she worked hard to identify her various pieces of armor, particular ways she had sought to cover both her pain and the vulnerable, tender heart beneath: food, busyness, personal perfectionism, her drivenness in her career, and even the ways she pushed her children to succeed.

Sharon saw yet more in her own story as she continued to speak it aloud. "You know, it is so ironic," she said, "but I think fatigue—the endpoint of all that busyness—was my biggest chunk of armor. I was too tired to have friends, too tired to answer questions, too tired for sex, too tired to play, and too tired to grieve. I was too tired to enjoy my own life." A full year had passed since this healing work of God had begun in Sharon's life, yet as we spoke, I could still sense her sadness as she grieved all that her busyness had cost her.

As Sharon surrendered piece after piece of armor, layer upon layer of beauty was revealed. She was grateful for a sustained and powerful sense of no longer wanting to hide the woman beneath the armor. Intuitively, she knew that her avoidance of her fragile but strong feminine soul was the real reason she had hung on to all those heavy pieces of protection for so long. Her renewed vision of her own beauty enabled her to let go of her familiar and restrictive old habits.

Daring to be still is a core struggle for many, many women. In my work as a chaplain, I often meet women in the hospital who have been forced into stillness by sickness. Many struggle with strong feelings of worthlessness and emptiness when the busyness of their lives is no more. It is as if the activity of motion alone creates within them their only sense of substance as women. Once the activity has ceased, their sense of self seems to evaporate, leaving only a painful void. Though frightening, such experiences are often the first step toward healing and the flowering of their uniquely feminine souls.

The grace of such an invitation to stop running comes in many forms. For some it is illness. For Sharon it was her husband's gift of a weekend alone. For Martha it was an encounter with Jesus Himself.

AN ANCIENT WOMAN'S SOUL

It is difficult to imagine the life of Jesus on earth with any sense of daily reality. What was it like moment to moment? What made Him laugh? What foods did He like best? How much sleep did He get every night? Where did He go when He needed some downtime?

Though we cannot answer many of these questions, we do know that He considered the siblings Martha, Mary, and Lazarus to be friends and their home to be a place of welcome. The Gospel writers used the stories of Jesus' encounters with these two sisters in particular to give us a glimpse of how Jesus related to women.

As is almost always true of sisters, these women were very different in temperament, giftedness, and struggle. In Luke 10:38-42, the first of two scenes where we see both women, Jesus used that difference to highlight for us "good" versus "better" choices. Though in recent years I have heard teaching that moves away from interpreting Martha's choices as "less," Jesus' words seem to be clear.

Martha's unique and significant struggles ring very true for me. I can learn from her pain without "demonizing" her because I *am* her.

A Daring Graciousness

As Jesus and his disciples were on their way, he came to a village where a woman named Martha opened her home to him. (verse 38)

From the start, we see that Martha was quite a woman. The Gospel writer refers to the home as hers rather than as the home of Lazarus, an unusual distinction for the culture of that day. As Jesus traveled the region, He did not have the option of inns but had to rely on those who might dare to house Him. Because Jesus was a controversial Rabbi, it was probably not an easy decision for those such as Martha, Mary, and Lazarus, who were significantly connected with their Jewish community. Opening her home to Jesus was an act of faith and courage Martha could never have predicted would end up being so personally disruptive.

A Radical Choice

She had a sister called Mary, who sat at the Lord's feet listening to what he said. (verse 39)

At first glance, Mary's choice appears much more passive than Martha's invitation. But look again. Though Martha's choice of guest reflected her daring, her role as a hostess was expected and socially acceptable. Mary, however, in taking her seat at the foot of a rabbi, was making a socially radical choice: the choice to learn. Though men were granted that privilege, women were not.

Not only was her choice to sit radical, but she also dared to let go of the other expected tasks. For most women, this is a far greater battle. We foolishly think we can do it all. My guess is that she was just as aware as Martha of all that needed to be done; she simply let it go in order to grasp something more. I would imagine that though her exterior may have been calm in the moment, her soul was battling both accusing looks around her and critical voices within.

Deceptive Distractions

But Martha was distracted by all the preparations that had to be made. (verse 40)

When we address issues of distraction in our lives, we tend to focus on the object causing our distraction as the problem. However, the troublesome truth is that we will never be free from potential distractions. The reality is that almost anything in our lives can become a distraction because what makes it so is not the essence of the object but how we use it in our lives. For example, I can use food to fuel my body, or I can use it to distract myself from the pain of a fight with my daughter. I can use worship songs to connect with God, or I can use them to try to soothe my frazzled soul instead of facing the real issues behind my distress. Distractions are always available. Wisdom asks not only, "What are my distractions?" but, more critically, "What am I distracted from? Whom or what is it I am running from?"

Think of how the word *distraction* can be broken down: *dis* meaning "not" and *traction* meaning "grip" or "contact sufficient to allow forward motion." So to be distracted could mean simply being out of touch with our own lives. Our inner world becomes disconnected from our outer world. We begin to lose traction and spin in place, unable to move forward. Perhaps we become distracted as a subtle way of avoiding something directly in our path.

But what would Martha have been avoiding? The simple answer might be intimate relationship with Jesus. As we learned from the woman at the well, intimacy is often a tough choice. Though our souls thirst for it, there is risk involved. Our choice to open ourselves to relationship with another, even with God, is far from automatic.

But is that all? Like my friend Sharon, I think Martha had her own suit of armor: doing good. Like Sharon, Martha might have feared that there was no one beneath the armor, no woman apart from the "faithful servant." She had been busily serving for so long that it may have felt as if "the one who busily serves" was her only source of identity. To sit at the feet of Jesus would have meant opening the door to a new understanding of herself and a deeper understanding of her feminine soul.

Martha clung to her long list of have-to's, at least in part, to cover a life full of vulnerably frightening human needs and desires. She may have been running from her own sense of need for Jesus, her own sense of delight in His presence, her own longing for the kind of intimacy Mary was drawn to and was willing to risk so much to obtain. She fled from the truth of her own feminine soul as well as intimate relationship with Jesus. She fled into a life of doing.

The needed preparations were real. Urgent. Demanding. They were for Jesus' benefit. Yet they also kept her out of touch with her own desires and kept Jesus at arm's length. Though hospitality at times can flow from an intimate connection, we do not get that sense from this passage. Here, Martha's service seems to be an offering of hands rather than heart. This can be the "dark side" of our feminine souls' wonderful bent toward hospitality, where the good becomes the enemy of the best.

Revealing Resentments

She came to him and asked, "Lord, don't you care that my sister has left me to do the work by myself? Tell her to help me!" (verse 40)

Did you catch that Martha went to Jesus, not to Mary? At first glance, we tend to assume that her relational struggle was with Mary. Here, however, her accusation was not against Mary but against Jesus for not caring for her, not providing the help she needed. This woman who had chosen for herself a life of "doing" over an opportunity for "being" in relationship felt misused. Could it be that she did not experience Jesus' care because she would not let her feminine soul be cared for by Him?

Truth be told, this is a huge problem for us as women. Most of us struggle to accept a simple compliment, much less real care. We also are often blind to how we repeatedly set ourselves up to experience neglect. Though Mary had physically put herself in a receiving posture, Martha had not. Her unbending role as dutiful servant was a bad habit. The idea of having legitimate feminine needs or being with Jesus as a beloved friend was nowhere in the picture. This is one of those backward, upside-down, in-a-mirror moments of feminine soul dynamics. True repentance might appear very nontraditional, perhaps even as radical as giving up the role of dutiful servant for a few moments of receiving care.

Ironically, though Martha's accusation was against Jesus, her resentment focused on Mary. Could it be that Martha was angry with Mary because she had acknowledged and chosen what Martha herself so longed for: to be cared for by Jesus? As is often the case, the target of her resentment revealed the hidden longing of her own heart.

It makes me sad to see that Martha did not come to Jesus with her legitimate and vulnerable desire to be nurtured; instead, she came with a demand. Her resentment was simply another way to run from her feminine soul and a vulnerably honest relationship with Jesus. Under the armor of a plea for justice was a heart longing for the very thing she had denied herself.

Acknowledging Reality

"Martha, Martha," the Lord answered, "you are worried and upset about many things." (verse 41)

Jesus did not rebuke, correct, or shame Martha. Neither did He follow her command to rebuke Mary. Can you hear the grief and love in Jesus' voice? He began to care for Martha's soul. She said, "Don't you care?" He said, "I see you and know you even better than you know yourself." Now that she had chosen to engage Him, even in her anger and accusation, He offered her what she needed even more than justice or help in the kitchen: nurturing.

Jesus began by naming for Martha her personal reality, inviting her to be more aware of her long-neglected feminine soul. He confronted her with herself, her pain and suffering. She had chosen to focus on her busyness and the behavior of others so that she could not see herself. He saw and spoke her pain, inviting her to own her self-inflicted anxiety. In so doing, Jesus demonstrated His absolute embrace of her fractured, hurting, and resentful soul. He met her in the reality of where she was and invited her to live more presently with her painful internal truth.

Self-awareness is a significant struggle for many women. Flight from ourselves and flight from God are very closely related. We often need supernatural help to break through our long-standing habits of self-forgetfulness and false self-perceptions. Jesus makes sure we know that help is available. Even now, He longs to nurture our stubbornly busy feminine souls.

Birthing a New Perspective

"But only one thing is needed." (verse 42)

Isn't it curious that Jesus did not name the "one thing" for us? Maybe He knew that if He did, the "Martha" in us all would make a formula and to-do list of what He never intended to be such. He left us instead with an image of busy, distracted, worried, upset, resentful Martha and still, seated, waiting, willing to be hungry, freer from social expectations, focused Mary. But is this image the only way to define the "one thing"?

Maybe Jesus knew that this "one thing" is beyond what words can explain. The opportunity for the kind of intimate connection with Christ that Mary chose had less to do with activity or lack thereof and more to do with a heart's willingness to need what a heart needs most. It is frightening to acknowledge that we desperately need that which we cannot control, that which we cannot provide in any way for ourselves. It is maddening to wait in stillness and longing.

These moments of deep intimacy with God cannot be scripted. They take many unexpected shapes and forms: ducks landing on a lake at sunset, the smile of a baby, a Scripture story offering the needed wisdom for a moment, prayer, a hymn, a hug, bread and wine. They come as delightful surprises and winsome grace, like an unexpected visit from a precious friend.

The tough thing is that our call is to live the course of our lives with hearts open, full of longing, and continually aware of the "one thing." We are called to not fill our lives so full of distractions that when the moment of grace comes, we miss it, having mistaken our distractions for life itself.

Choosing the Good Part

"Mary has chosen what is better [literally, the "good part"], and it will not be taken away from her." (verse 42)

Recall Martha's plea to Jesus: "Tell her to help me!" Jesus answered her as He affirmed Mary's choice: He would not take away from Mary the joy of learning and the delight of intentionally receiving the nurturing presence of Christ. She dared to take a seat, and He blessed her choice, defending her against the less than subtle accusations of her sister.

Unfortunately, it is often those closest to us who are most disturbed when we make the daring choice to sit with Jesus. Understandably, they are accustomed to our help and our service, and it is a genuine loss for them. But note: Jesus did not choose to protect Martha from that loss of help; instead, He invited her to join Mary.

Certainly Martha was right: The need for work was real. Supper might not get done. We as women have an internal drive and a very real calling to serve others. They depend on our nurturing spirits rightly. Such a noble calling, though, sets us up for Martha's particular struggle. We forget that service to others is neither our only nor our highest calling.

Jesus invited Martha to a fuller understanding of her feminine soul. Part of discovering that wisdom was the simple recognition that there was a choice involved. In Martha's thinking, there was no choice, only one right thing. Her mind was filled with imperative thoughts, dictating her life as a series of automatic responses to all the unexamined shoulds, musts, have-to's, and ought-to's in her head. She saw both herself and her relationship with Jesus too narrowly. Jesus wanted Martha to see that she was more than a servant, so much more than "one who busily serves." She was a woman with valid needs of her own. Without condemning her choice to serve and nurture, He let her know she could make different choices that pleased Him even more.

As He affirmed Mary, He legitimized for Martha an alternative way to live: the "good part." As is so often God's way with women, rather than seeking to drive her away from something that was "less" with rebuke, Jesus drew Martha with something "more," something beautiful. Jesus gently lured her toward the healing, restoration, and growth of her feminine soul.

But in order to receive the "more," Martha had to let go of the "less." She had to choose to stop running. Rarely in life can we have it all. This is a hard truth to absorb for those of us constantly bombarded by a consumerist culture that entices us to gluttony of all kinds—including gluttony of life experiences. Jesus invited Martha to release her busyness for a moment and receive the nurturing presence of God. He invited her to let go of the false sense of pleasing Him by earning her way through service and to simply receive the grace of His presence.

I am sad to say that the story stops here. We are left without a sense of Martha's response. But, believing real change is possible, I like to imagine a deep sigh of ease and relief that might have spread over Martha's face as she took her place beside her sister. And who knows, maybe Jesus had His other disciples—His male disciples—cook dinner that night!

Both Martha of Bethany and my friend Sharon continue to inspire me. Sharon's life is different now. Many in her church community are quite disturbed by decisions she has made to pull out of various activities over time. Her family is thankful for but also struggling with the change. Sharon has quit running, both from God and from herself. She told me the other day that when her life does get busy, she often hears God's gentle, inviting question, first offered in the Garden of Eden (see Genesis 3:9): "Sharon, where are you?" She remarked that that's not the sort of question one can answer on the fly. The glow on her face is remarkable as she radiates with the affirmation of Jesus. The woman beneath the armor is beautiful and growing more so every day. Hey, maybe there is a fountain of youth after all!

YOUR JOURNEY

For personal reflection and group discussion

1. If the pace of your life were calibrated *like* the speed of a car, what would you estimate your average miles per hour to be during this past week? Explain your answer.

2. Recall the last time you spent the day totally alone with yourself and God, either by choice or circumstance. Describe the experience, both externally (circumstances and actions) and internally (feelings and responses).

3. Choosing to be open (physically, emotionally, or spiritually) is always risky. How open to Jesus do you

feel right now? Which areas are easiest to open to Him? Which are most difficult?

4. Picture yourself seated at Jesus' feet. Take five minutes to be still, imagining your whole being opening to the person of Christ. Describe your experience.

5. What behaviors do you run to when you are avoiding yourself or intimacy with God? What is your willingness to be distracted costing you?

6. Explore a past or present resentment from your life. Is there a hidden longing in your heart—something you have denied yourself under the guise of faithfulness, unselfishness, or justice—that may be a legitimate desire of your feminine soul?

7. Take the next five minutes to write nonstop (in a stream-of-consciousness approach) your own personal list of things that worry and upset you. Nothing is too big or too small for the list. Own for yourself Jesus' words of compassion for Martha.

8. Describe an experience of intimacy with God. Try to put words to your need for God. How can you live more fully open to the "one thing" that is needed?

9. Recall any experiences in which those close to you criticized you for daring to make the choice to sit for a while. How did you respond externally? Internally? Can you hear Jesus defending you?

10. Like Martha, most of us view both our busyness and our time in general as out of our control. We say, "I just didn't have enough time," or we pray that God will stretch our time. Yet the reality is that for the most part we choose, albeit often unconsciously, how we spend our days, both in content and in pace. Owning your power to choose, how would you re-create your life? What mile-per-hour pace would you like to adopt? What steps will you take this week toward change? Every step counts, no matter how small it may seem at the time that you take it.

CHAPTER FOUR

Giving Up Words,
Daring to be Silent

MARY OF BETHANY IN JOHN 11

As women, we use words differently than men do, often less directly. Though seemingly meant for connection, the words women use can act as a wall, hiding the most vulnerable parts of themselves. If we, with Mary, dare silence, Jesus will meet us in surprising and healing ways.

To Consider . . .

In times of stress, we all have our own ways of coping. How do you tend to cope with sudden disruptions in your life? In those moments of stress, how do you use language? How do you respond to silence?

HER mother's sudden heart attack came as quite a shock to Donna. They had just enjoyed a wonderfully rich time together over the Christmas break, and my friend was headed back to her home just across the state line when she got the call. Her mother was in the intensive care unit on a breathing machine and was not expected to live through the night.

As I walked into the dark, quiet room, my friend's grief was so large it filled the whole space. Donna sat stiffly in a small chair, quietly beside her mother, holding her hand. From time to time she glanced at the adjacent machine with its lighted dials and gentle rhythmic motions, seeking to somehow use that soft rhythm to knead these painful and unfamiliar realities into her soul.

She looked up as I entered, her eyes full of tears. Remaining frozen in her chair, she whispered, "How do I do this? What do I do now?" Her voice shook with grief and profound uncertainty, clearly conveying feelings of being lost and confused, without a sense of ground.

On one level my friend was simply seeking advice. She was in shock, trying to find her bearings and needing help locating herself in a world that was filled with sudden change, pain, and emotional chaos. In her pain and trauma, Donna had temporarily forgotten who she was as a woman of strength and faith. She had lost touch with her feminine soul.

As women in crisis often do, she was desperately looking outside of herself for a way to fix her life and end her pain. Though comfort from the outside world made a difference in the moment, the wisdom she needed was beyond words. She sought a wisdom of the heart that dwelt only within her own soul. In that moment, words, theories, and advice would only have distracted from the internal listening Donna needed to do.

As a hospital chaplain, I have been with hundreds of people in similar moments when the trauma and pain of life were far beyond words. Holy silence is often the most healing response yet the most difficult to dare. The same silence that magnifies our sense of God's comforting presence also seems to magnify our pain.

For Donna, to listen to her own soul right then would have also meant being present to the agonizing sense of loss that dwelt within. It would have required an unusual courage. As I wept with her, I offered her confident assurance that only she knew how to use these last moments with her dear mother. She knew her mother well and loved her fiercely. "Listen to your heart," I said. "You'll know what to do."

Over the next week, Donna did just that. Though her mother never regained consciousness, she could be taken off the breathing machine and moved to a private room. Donna felt the impact of that move. She grieved intensely in those first few days, crying more tears than she had dreamed possible. This was to be the room in which her mother would die.

The vigil was a holy one. As they settled into the more comfortable space, Donna's grief seemed to take on a more active expression. At times, my friend read to her mom. She finished a book of poetry her mother had recently begun reading. She read the Bible. She sang to her mother. She bought her fancy pajamas, did her hair, and bathed her body. She visited with friends and family, telling story after story of her mother's long, rich, and full life. A few days later, Donna began to relax into the silence of her mother's room. She sat with her in the quiet, listening. Hour upon hour of silent listening.

As I visited with Donna later that week at her mom's bedside, I was surprised at her peace and joy. I was amazed to hear her say, "Even now she's teaching me—about silence, about stillness, about waiting, about listening." Wisely letting go of words, wisely engaging the silence, her feminine soul heard more deeply and more completely, connecting with her mother, herself, and God in new soul-expanding ways too deep for words.

Reading again recently the story of Mary of Bethany, I realized that she, too, had experienced Donna's courageous choice of silence.

AN ANCIENT WOMAN'S SOUL

This second story of Jesus' relationship with Mary and Martha in John 11 reveals even more about His deep love for them. Again we see much through contrast.

The Silence of God

Now a man named Lazarus was sick. He was from Bethany, the village of Mary and her sister Martha. This Mary, whose brother Lazarus now lay sick, was the same one who poured perfume on the Lord and wiped his feet with her hair. So the sisters sent word to Jesus, "Lord, the one you love is sick."

When he heard this, Jesus said, "This sickness will not end in death. No, it is for God's glory so that God's Son may be glorified through it." Jesus loved Martha and her sister and Lazarus. Yet when he heard that Lazarus was sick, he stayed where he was two more days.

Then he said to his disciples, "Let us go back to Judea."

"But Rabbi," they said, "a short while ago the Jews tried to stone you, and yet you are going back there?"

Jesus answered, "Are there not twelve hours of daylight? A man who walks by day will not stumble, for he sees by this world's light. It is when he walks by night that he stumbles, for he has no light."

After he had said this, he went on to tell them, "Our friend Lazarus has fallen asleep; but I am going there to wake him up."

His disciples replied, "Lord, if he sleeps, he will get better." Jesus had been speaking of his death, but his disciples thought he meant natural sleep.

So then he told them plainly, "Lazarus is dead, and for your sake I am glad I was not there, so that you may believe. But let us go to him."

Then Thomas (called Didymus) said to the rest of the disciples, "Let us also go, that we may die with him." (verses 1-16)

Some tragedies in life are beyond explanation: Innocent children are abused, whole nations are exterminated, a mother dies in a car accident simply because she was in the wrong place at the wrong time. We experience God as strangely silent in the face of our pain and questions. In fact, at times we begin to feel invisible, forgotten by the God of the universe. And we wonder, *What must God be thinking? Who is this God I serve anyway?*

Mary and Martha must have felt forgotten by God in the days surrounding their brother's death. As far as we know, Jesus was silent toward them. Yet in this story we get a rare glimpse behind the scenes in a moment of God's silence. First, Jesus had a vision for good in the midst of the suffering: "It is for God's glory." Their suffering was not random but purposeful. Second, we are explicitly reminded, "Jesus loved Martha and her sister and Lazarus." Whatever else God's silence might have meant, it did not mean He did not love them. Third, Jesus was aware of them and had a plan, initiating movement toward them when the time was right. They were most certainly not forgotten.

Faith and Accusation

On his arrival, Jesus found that Lazarus had already been in the tomb for four days. Bethany was less than two miles from Jerusalem, and many Jews had come to Martha and Mary to comfort them in the loss of their brother. When Martha heard that Jesus was coming, she went out to meet him, but Mary stayed at home.

"Lord," Martha said to Jesus, "if you had been here, my brother would not have died." (verses 17-21)

Martha's initial words to Jesus are identical to Mary's, seen later in our text. The repetition makes them especially meaningful for us. Though we tend to read these words as if they are a question for Jesus, they are technically a statement. In Martha's and Mary's words, we sense both great faith and the sting of accusation. They had unwavering confidence that if Jesus had come, He could have healed their brother: great faith. They also knew He had not come, and the strength of their statement called for an answer, an accounting for His lack of response.

Clearly both women were confused. This silent God was a new experience for them, raising legitimate and difficult questions, disrupting their whole image of this healing prophet and friend.

Their experience did not fit their understanding of this God-man. They were, in a word, disillusioned. Their present image of Jesus was no longer fact but an illusion, a false image that had to be destroyed before a new understanding could be created. In the midst of such destruction, there was chaos and pain, a loss of their very "ground." The grief of their brother's death was multiplied by this additional trauma. They had not only lost their brother, but it felt as if they had lost Jesus, too.

Coping with Words

> *"But I know that even now God will give you whatever you ask."*
>
> *Jesus said to her, "Your brother will rise again."*
>
> *Martha answered, "I know he will rise again in the resurrection at the last day."*
>
> *Jesus said to her, "I am the resurrection and the life. He who believes in me will live, even though he dies; and whoever lives and believes in me will never die. Do you believe this?"*
>
> *"Yes, Lord," she told him, "I believe that you are the Christ, the Son of God, who was to come into the world."*
>
> *And after she had said this, she went back and called her sister Mary aside. "The Teacher is here," she said, "and is asking for you." (verses 22-28)*

Many scholars have interpreted this exchange between Jesus and Martha in various ways.[1] At first glance, the words sound wonderfully profound, full of faith and meaning. Yet if we look more closely, we may see the conversation differently.

First, this encounter with Martha was only words—no record of body language or emotion at all. That fact has even more significance when we contrast it with Mary's encounter later in this passage. Second, Martha seems to have been speaking but not really conversing with Jesus. Though Jesus was telling her what she most wanted to hear (that Lazarus would be raised), she remained caught in distant theory, unable to imagine the hope for that moment. And finally, though her confession of Jesus as the Christ seems huge, the scene shifted immediately without any comment or response, deemphasizing her confession. (For contrast, note Jesus' strong reinforcement of Peter's very similar confession in Matthew 16:13-19.)

These observations, along with Martha's comment at the tomb (explored a bit later), indicate that for Martha, words in this moment might have been more of a coping mechanism to try to order her world than an opportunity for connection with Jesus. Though the words appear logical and rational, they have no problem-solving efficacy. Perhaps the noise of her voice numbed the pain for a moment. Noise can be an effective, albeit temporary, anesthetic.

When our lives are filled with pain and chaos, we do the best we can. For Martha, that meant words. Unfortunately, she was possibly too pained and frightened to bring her whole self, her feminine soul, to Jesus for comfort. Bringing what she could, Martha sought to deal intellectually with all that had happened, and Jesus met her there. He joined her in the realm of words and concepts, again without shame, rebuke, or accusation. He offered her what she could receive.

Sadly, we have no indication that she received much comfort from this verbal exchange. Her inability to bring herself more completely and authentically to the moment cut her off from the full experience of all Jesus sought to give. Even to the end, the tone of the passage feels mechanical. Words seem to be more a wall than a door.

Connecting Beyond Words

When Mary heard this, she got up quickly and went to him. Now Jesus had not yet entered the village, but was still at the place where Martha had met him. When the Jews who had been with Mary in the house, comforting her, noticed how quickly she got up and went out, they followed her, supposing she was going to the tomb to mourn there.

When Mary reached the place where Jesus was and saw him, she fell at his feet and said, "Lord, if you had been here, my brother would not have died."

When Jesus saw her weeping, and the Jews who had come along with her also weeping, he was deeply moved in spirit and troubled. "Where have you laid him?" he asked.

"Come and see, Lord," they replied.

Jesus wept.

Then the Jews said, "See how he loved him!"

But some of them said, "Could not he who opened the eyes of the blind man have kept this man from dying?" (verses 29-37)

Did you notice the shift in tone? Mary got up quickly. Mary saw Jesus. Mary fell at His feet and wept. She also brought a whole community of folks with her. A much different scene. Apart from the opening words that both women uttered, we have no record of any words spoken by Mary.

The sense I get from both the absence of words and the presence of the descriptors in this passage is that rather than seeking an escape or solution to the chaos and pain of the moment, Mary simply experienced her grief and confusion as fully as possible. She lived present to her whole self: physically, emotionally, spiritually, intellectually. She brought her feminine soul to the feet of Jesus. Words could never have expressed all that moment contained, so she let go of them. Her heart was an open wound, and she made no move to cover it.

Amid her silent pain and deep vulnerability, we see a strong response from and connection with Jesus. He was profoundly moved in spirit and wept with Mary. Though there was no conversation between Mary and Jesus, much was heard by her. Messages deeper and broader than words were communicated in those few moments. Again, Jesus allowed the woman to set the tone. Mary's choice of greater vulnerability reaped a reward of deeper connection and more profound comfort.

It is important to note that Jesus knew He was about to raise Lazarus. Logically, there was no reason for tears or distress. Yet Jesus knew that logic was not even close to the whole reality, especially for Mary's feminine soul. Jesus' choice was significant. His tears in this moment affirmed Mary's deeply and understandably emotional response to her brother's death. His choice to share her tears even when He could have "resolved" them with logic honored the goodness of her emotional experience of the world. Jesus did not live in the future, in the comfort of theory and theology. He lived in the present, emotional and painful as it was, sharing Mary's tears and honoring well her feminine soul.

The Challenge of Hearing God

Jesus, once more deeply moved, came to the tomb. It was a cave with a stone laid across the entrance. "Take away the stone," he said.

"But, Lord," said Martha, the sister of the dead man, "by this time there is a bad odor, for he has been there four days."

Then Jesus said, "Did I not tell you that if you believed, you would see the glory of God?"

So they took away the stone. Then Jesus looked up and said, "Father, I thank you that you have heard me. I knew that you always hear me, but I said this for the benefit of the people standing here, that they may believe that you sent me."

When he had said this, Jesus called in a loud voice, "Lazarus, come out!" The dead man came out, his hands and feet wrapped with strips of linen, and a cloth around his face.

Jesus said to them, "Take off the grave clothes and let him go."
(verses 38-44)

As they approached the grave, again Martha began speaking. Her concerns seem to indicate she had heard little in her previous exchange with Jesus. She was told her brother would rise again, but she was worried about rotting flesh. She was told she would see God's glory, yet she sought to stop Jesus for fear of a bad smell.

Jesus' words to her tried to help her recognize that she had not listened well during their earlier conversation. She had forgotten what He had said, or perhaps she had never really heard. Again, all those wonderful theological words had not increased connection; ironically, they may even have prevented it from happening at all.

We live in a word-dominated world today. Without realizing it, many times we invalidate anything we cannot name. Yet this story of Mary and the story of my friend Donna speak of powerful moments of connection and learning even in the absence of language. Though clearly these profound "beyond words" kinds of moments happen to both sexes, my experience and stories such as this one from Scripture have told me that the feminine soul has a special gift for seeing and listening to these wordless connections.

It is unfortunate that we as women often discount these experiences because we cannot fully share them with others in traditional or easily understood ways. Some of the most meaningful, soul-shaping times of our lives become invisible to us, their power and significance lost for want of words.

I invite you to become more aware of how you use words, as well as how you respond to silence. Dare to reclaim some of those times of "beyond words" transformation, putting whatever words you can to them—if you so choose—but steadfastly refusing to disempower them if they are simply beyond what language can express.

YOUR JOURNEY

For personal reflection and group discussion

1. How do you use language when you are stressed? Do you babble, talking a lot without saying anything? Do you analyze and problem solve? Do you let off emotional steam?

2. Have you ever experienced the silence of God in the midst of hard times? Describe both the external circumstances and your internal experience.

3. Imagine the story behind that silence, as if someone were interviewing Jesus as He waited for the right moment to break the silence. How would He speak of His vision for glory, His love for you, His moment-by-moment awareness, and His initiative of a plan for good? Describe what you can imagine.

4. Have you ever been through a season of disillusionment in your relationship with Jesus? Describe your understanding of God before and after this season.

5. Can you think of a time when you used words more as a wall than as a way to welcome connection with another person? Have you ever used noise to numb your pain?

6. When your life is full of hurt and chaos, what do you tend to want from your relationship with God? Do you look for theological answers? Mystical experiences? Right responses? Something else?

7. Have you ever dared to fall at the feet of Jesus weeping? In that moment, did you sense Him weeping with you or some other response on His part?

8. What meaningful connections have you made in silence?

9. What are the moments in your life that are beyond words? How do you share those moments? Do you struggle to hold on to their power because of the challenge of naming them?

10. Is there some part of your being that needs the healing that can come only in silence? What will you do this week to honor this need of your feminine soul?

Part Two

FEMININE SOULS IN TRANSITION

CHAPTER FIVE

Choosing Our Healing,
Growing Our Faith

THE WOMAN WITH A HEMORRHAGE IN LUKE 8:43-48

Though Jesus' male disciples were often rebuked
for their tendency toward self-assertion, the
women in His life struggled to advocate for their
own needs and growth. Do we as women really
want to be whole? Have we forgotten our part in
the process, disowning the need to make choices
that evidence our faith? As the woman with a
hemorrhage courageously acted on her faith, Jesus
provided all she needed for life-transforming
growth. In fact, He invited her to an even deeper
healing than she herself had dared to imagine.

To Consider . . .

In what areas of your life do you need God's healing touch?

I KNEW I was in bad shape that morning. For one thing, I simply could not sit still. The sunny spring day outside belied the storm brewing in my soul. The children were off at school, and I was nervously getting the house ready for a Bible study I would be leading for some women from my church. Or at least that was my plan.

That very issue—would I lead or not?—was the subject of an intense and ongoing argument I had been having with God since the day before when I accompanied a hurting friend to a counselor's office. I had referred many others to counseling, but I had never sensed the need for it myself. To this day I do not know if it was a supernatural urging by the Holy Spirit or the counselor's acute discernment from our few phone conversations, but for some reason he handed me a copy of a magazine article to read. Prompted more by curiosity than by any conscious emotional pain, I read it as soon as I got home. And thus began my wrestling with God.

Hardly anyone, including the counselor, knew that since the previous autumn I had been exploring some new personal insights I happened upon almost by accident. They came in the form of a book I was reading to help a teenage neighbor. One of my friends had recommended Dan Allender's *The Wounded Heart* to help me understand this young woman's struggles. Little did I know that I would recognize so many of my own patterns in those pages.

Over that fall and winter as I read and reflected, I began to see and own the fact that I was the ultimate competent woman. While that might be a good thing for many women, for me competence was mostly a self-protective mask. Instead of feeling, I functioned. Rather than grieving, I evaluated and judged. Instead of hurting, I analyzed and intellectualized my pain. Rather than acknowledging my human needs, I pretended to have none. Refusing to reveal my tenderness, I projected a tough exterior.

My ability to perform well in my highly efficient, mechanistic sort of way had worked for decades to protect my feminine soul from feeling need or being hurt. Now, for the first time, all my "driven doing good for God" was beginning to take on a new, darker meaning. Though I am confident that on some level God had used my years of good work to bless others, something big and important was missing—though sadly I had no idea what it was.

Slowly, I was becoming more and more aware that my mask was not only protecting me from harm but also keeping good things out of my life. As I questioned my false sense of personhood, I became even more puzzled by the fact that I had no sense of the *true* me. I was so adept at hiding that I had managed to hide even from myself.

As autumn became winter and winter awoke to spring, I continued to be intrigued by these new insights. I now understood my own life story, behavior, and choices more, but oddly, my emotions remained relatively unmoved. I began to imagine what healing might look like for me, how my life would change if I owned my neediness and tenderness. Still, all my imagining remained an abstract idea, a passive hope. I had no idea where or how to begin.

The article the counselor gave me was the personal story of a woman who struggled with the same mask of competence I had identified in my life. As I read about the details of her story and the depth of her pain, I began to feel my own for the first time. This work of God in my life transitioned from intriguing ideas to heart-wrenching emotion: anger, grief, brokenness.

But suffering and pain were not the only things spelled out in that article. This courageous woman's healing journey was detailed: one frightening, painful, and life-giving choice at a time. Until now, all my insight had been passive, free of the burden of choice. But as I contemplated her story more deeply, I felt waves of terror washing over my soul. To change privately behind my mask was one thing, to give it up altogether quite another. Though the past nine months had been a critical time of growth and insight for me, I had told very few people in my life about any of my thoughts and feelings. To let the world around me see and know those very tender parts of my wounded heart and vulnerable soul was frightening beyond words. But like it or not, that was the direction this path was headed. The question beat loudly in my chest: Would I, like the woman in the article, choose healing?

That question first presented itself as a specific choice while I prepared my living room for the ladies' Bible study, setting up the white board, unpacking the markers. I had awakened that day with a great sense of heaviness from the wrestling and pain of the evening before. "I can't be needy *now!*" I argued with God. "These women are counting on me. There might be visitors, women who need to hear the gospel. It would just be selfish."

As I ranted, God seemed to listen patiently. Unexpectedly, a face came to mind. It was the face of a woman I had known many years before, a prominent Sunday school teacher in a church we had once attended. She, too, was a competent woman. Her competence was the only truth most people ever knew about her life. Yet through a series of unique circumstances beyond her control, God had given me private glimpses into the tragic relational realities of her life. I had seen firsthand the profound pain and sadness of destructive behavior such as uncontrolled rage, sexual abuse, and legalism coupled with determined denial and secrecy. Beneath pristine reputations and never-failing smiles, I witnessed fractured relationships and lives. Such brokenness comes to us all in some form, but for this prominent woman and those closest to her, the greater tragedy was that they could receive no help and comfort because no one knew their pain.

God made it clear to me that morning: The choice was mine. I could give up my mask of competence and opt for healing, or I could live out the sad drama of a woman whose hidden pain had nearly destroyed her. I felt both God's tender invitation and His unbending love for me. Though my options seemed clear, my choice did not. This struggle was deeply rooted in my soul; my fear of exposure and vulnerability were intense. Even as the doorbell rang, I did not know what I would choose.

When the women arrived at my house, I began the Bible study as planned. A few minutes into it, however, I could no longer pretend. Taking the greatest leap of faith of my life up to that point, I threw down my whiteboard marker and wailed, "I can't do this anymore. I'm too needy." I hung my head, covered my face, and sobbed.

Though I can still feel the pain and terror of that moment, I have never regretted my choice. Dropping the safety and invisibility of my mask of competence and letting the world come to know Janet has been a long series of transforming but terrifying choices, including starting counseling. When I made my first appointment, I had no idea of the magnitude of healing God was beginning to work within me. Fortunately, God once again gave me a faithful companion for the journey, a mentor of old who also chose the healing path.

AN ANCIENT WOMAN'S SOUL

Many of the stories of women in the Gospels are brief vignettes offered to us by the Gospel writers, highlighting Jesus' relationships with women. The narrative of the woman with the hemorrhage in Luke 8:42-48 is one such story. In spite of its brevity, the historical account holds many clear and powerfully affirming messages for women. It also reflects Jesus' astute understanding of our feminine souls' penchant for hiding.

The Busyness of God

As Jesus was on his way, the crowds almost crushed him. (verse 42)

This woman's story of healing has an unusual place in the gospel of Luke. It is actually sandwiched in the middle of another healing event. In the preceding verses we learn that Jesus had just returned to this area, and the people were waiting for Him, welcoming Him. A ruler of the synagogue, Jairus, was especially anxious for His arrival and began to plead with Him to come and heal his dying daughter, his only daughter. As Jesus set out on His way to meet this pressing need, the woman with the hemorrhage interrupted the intended plans of God.

Have you ever felt as if you were interrupting God? This unique context invites us to consider our particular perspective on the busyness of God. Though intellectually we reject the idea, many women live in a functional relationship with God that assumes God is too busy to be bothered with much of what concerns them. Though God does not trivialize our unique concerns, needs, pains, and woundedness, we trivialize ourselves on God's behalf.

In seeking to avoid our pain, we often diminish our hurts and suffering. We let the very real and seemingly competing needs of others continually push ours to the side. Trying to push our way through the crowd of needs that surround us, we never quite make it to the place where ours can be seen or heard. The overuse of our wonderful gift of nurturing becomes a tool of self-avoidance and eventually self-destruction.

But we do not stop there. We then project that diminishing perspective onto God's view of us. Boldly and recklessly daring to speak for God, we call ourselves "wimp" and "whiny," trying to shame the pain and grief from our own souls. We put our suffering on a comparative scale with starving orphans in Africa and try to convince ourselves that the daily aches we feel are nothing. We dare to assume that God is too busy with more pressing needs. Yet Jesus clearly demonstrates in this precious narrative that God is never too busy or overwhelmed to hear our story of need or pain.

In a world where people have not consistently taken the necessary time to care for us well, it is a challenge to hold on to the fact that God is different. As this story unfolds, we see repeatedly that Jesus took all the time necessary for the most complete kind of healing possible for this woman, caring for parts of her feminine soul she was not even aware needed His touch.

Enduring Woundedness

And a woman was there who had been subject to bleeding for twelve years, but no one could heal her. (verse 43)

One of the things I have learned in my years as a chaplain is that there are many different types of suffering in life, each with its own unique kind of pain. For instance, there is a pain from the suddenness of trauma that is not necessarily there with a cancer diagnosis. Yet with cancer, there is pain from fear associated with the word *cancer* that is not present in cases of trauma. Different kinds of suffering raise different challenges.

This woman's suffering was extended and chronic. For many, suffering of this kind becomes life defining. The very insistence of the pain reshapes the individual's self-concept. There is a good chance that this woman did not see herself as a *woman* who happened to have a certain medical condition but as a woman whose *life* was defined by her medical condition.

In this particular situation, that tendency toward redefinition of self was exacerbated by the social and religious implications of this woman's disease. According to Jewish law, anyone who was bleeding was considered unclean. Imagine twelve *years* of being unclean, unable to touch anyone without making him or her unclean also. Imagine being cut off from physical affection and public worship. In effect, society demanded that this woman be invisible. Imagine the loneliness and loss of hope.

Though certainly our customs are different today, many women continue to live in this same kind of agony. For example, victims of sexual abuse often have a powerful internal sense of feeling unclean. They, too, often suffer at the hands of a fearful society (and tragically even churches) that ignorantly labels them "unclean," refusing to touch their deep woundedness. Women who struggle with eating disorders, addiction, mental illness, or even infertility often hear the same destructive internal messages. Like this woman, their wounds can become life defining. Imagine the loneliness. Imagine the loss of hope.

Small Faith, Big Choice

She came up behind him and touched the edge of his cloak, and immediately her bleeding stopped. (verse 44)

Could you possibly come up with a smaller, more hidden, more hesitant description of touching Jesus? From *behind*, touching the *edge* of the *outer* garment. The fact that she should not have been in the crowd at all according to Jewish law undoubtedly factored into her choice of approaches. However, it may also provide evidence that she had internalized her socially imposed sense of diminishment and invisibility.

With faith as small as a mustard seed, this woman made the only choice needed for her healing. She reached out. She touched Jesus. The strength of *her* faith did not matter at all, only that of the One in whom she put her faith.

This first step of self-advocacy that moved her toward transformation does not fit our usual paradigm for growth. The most common path to a changed life put forth in many churches today emphasizes conviction, correction, and self-depreciation rather than self-concern, self-advocacy, and insight. Rarely are we willing to define repentance as choosing self-care over concern for others (for example, those who might be made unclean). Go figure.

On one hand, it was just a touch, a small act, simply another of many attempts to rid herself of this constant suffering. On the other hand, whether she realized it or not, it was a surrender of her whole identity, her whole way of being in the world, a pivotal choice in her life story. Often we dismiss the significance of a choice for healing. We think, *Of course people will opt to be healed.* Certainly that is usually true. But when becoming whole means leaving behind one's only sense of oneself, it can be unexpectedly terrifying.

That terror of life-altering change keeps many women locked in painful situations and immaturity. Consider the abused woman who will not leave her husband because she cannot imagine herself not married. Consider the career woman who longs to be home with her children but is afraid she might disappear as a person without her career. Consider the homemaker who yearns to go back to school but is afraid that such a choice might threaten the status quo at home or might even call into question her sense of personal identity or her public reputation as a "godly" wife and mother. Consider my argument with God that pivotal spring day as I struggled to let go of my mask of competence in front of a group of women who had come to my home to be led in Bible study.

Any choice for healing—real healing—is a leap of faith. Jesus did not miss this moment of great courage and faith. In fact, He expanded it. He wanted to heal this woman's feminine soul in more ways than she had bargained for.

Unfinished Business

"Who touched me?" Jesus asked. (verse 45)

It was an astonishing question—bordering on silly, it seems. As we were told, the crowd was almost crushing Jesus. Yet *He felt her touch*, one hurting, needy woman's timid brush against His hem. As we learn later, He felt the power leave Him. So why the question? Certainly there was no shortage of power, no need to be stingy or concerned with conservation. So what was the issue?

Jesus sensed some unfinished business. If bodily wholeness was His primary goal, His work was done. The author makes sure we know that she was healed before this point. There was no need for such a question. Yet He was not content with this woman's physical healing. Just as His earthly ministry was not primarily about physical healing but instead about restored relationship with God, this moment, too, was all about restoring relationship.

The way the healing happened—apart from relationship, cloaked in invisibility—told Jesus that a different kind of sickness was at work in this hidden recipient of His power. He understood that without a healing of the sense of self and dignity, the physical healing would bring little peace. He wanted more for this woman than she even knew to want for herself. Observe once again how Jesus' promotion of this woman is contrasted with His recurring need to rebuke His male disciples for self-promotion.

Jesus knows us uniquely as women, where we hurt and how we hide. He can be very determined while at the same time being utterly gentle. Watch as He ever so steadily draws her out, away from the shadows of invisibility.

Unhealed Wounds Exposed

When they all denied it, Peter said, "Master, the people are crowding and pressing against you." (verse 45)

The healed woman's choice to remain hidden in this moment confirms her need for further healing. As previously noted, the author makes sure we know that she was fully aware of her immediate physical healing (see verse 44). But though her body was whole, her soul was still shouting, "Unclean!" Her self-image had not changed. Rather than proclaiming her freedom and newness of life, she denied her faith and her healing. Rather than leaping and praising God as is noted of some of the men Jesus healed, she cowered, clinging to familiar invisibility.

As women, we tend to experience life in a more holistic and less compartmentalized way than men. Both our wounds and our healing seem to be more pervasive. For this woman, perhaps everything was happening too fast and she just needed time to absorb it all. Whatever her hesitancy, her faith had opened the door for change. Though she may have underestimated her need for further healing, Jesus did not.

Envisioning Enduring Wholeness

But Jesus said, "Someone touched me; I know that power has gone out from me." (verse 46)

Stubbornness can be an asset. Jesus was a bit persistent about His vision for this woman's lasting healing. Technically, He had given her a chance. He could have moved on. Instead, He gave her another chance, more time to make that critical second leap of faith.

Consider the scene around Him. The pressing crowd still there: smell, confusion, noise. Jairus' face: anxious, pleading, probably even angry. I am sure the synagogue ruler's choice to humble himself before Jesus and ask for help was not an easy one. His need was critical, urgent, and noble. His impatience seems justified. He had no idea what this Rabbi was waiting for. Should he leave now to be with his sick daughter as she died?

I am sure the disciples around Jesus were also annoyed. The synagogue leader was a man of status. He could do much for their cause. They, too, had no idea what Jesus was talking about. Still, Jesus persisted. He would not budge in His vision for the complete healing of this hurting woman's uniquely feminine soul.

More than any other single scene in Scripture, this image highlights Jesus' understanding of how critically important the issue of hiding is for the growth of women. Jesus maintained His focus for the good of the woman in the midst of both her resistance and all the pressures from men around Him who simply did not understand the unique needs of a woman or the importance of what was happening.

Though the church at large, men and women, may be limited in our understanding of feminine spirituality due to the predominantly taught masculine view, Jesus is not. He has worked in the lives of many women in this way all along. Often that healing work has been accomplished apart from or even in spite of the church rather than through it. As His sheep, some women have heard God's voice in unexpected places, at times in popular spirituality and feminism. God has sustained and grown them in creative and often nontraditional ways.

If we hear this story well, perhaps God is inviting us to begin to envision a better way. Imagine with me what it would be like for men and women to really digest stories such as this one and become more vocal about uniquely feminine spiritual struggles and needs. Imagine men recognizing these differences and advocating for these newly discovered needs in their churches. Imagine women refusing to resist Jesus' voice calling them out, away from the shadows of hiding. Imagine what it would be like if the whole church, men and women together, began to offer women this kind of healing. Imagine the healing power that could once again flow through Jesus' body, the church.

Invisibility Surrendered

Then the woman, seeing that she could not go unnoticed, came trembling and fell at his feet. In the presence of all the people, she told why she had touched him and how she had been instantly healed. (verse 47)

Confession time. This woman did not come forward wanting more healing. She had no idea she needed more. She came trembling, in fear and smallness in spite of the obvious miracle that had just been wrought in her body. Her body was free, but her soul was not.

She was not yet sure it was okay for her to be well, to be whole. On one hand that may sound absurd; on another it is very understandable. The place she had held in society for twelve years was no longer her place, and she had no idea where she fit. She simply did not know who she was or how to be well.

This new definition of self was the much-needed second healing. It was the reason Jesus persisted. It was the need no one but Jesus saw. It was the issue as urgent as the dying daughter of a synagogue ruler. Jesus knew that without the deeper healing of her feminine soul, this daughter of His would surely have died, too. Though the need for this healing of self is not exclusive to women, it does seem to be a special challenge for many of us.

As with Hannah's story, healing happened as this woman came to voice. She simply came and told her story. Jesus was wise, attentive, and persistent as He worked for her complete wholeness and freedom. Just as He did with this woman, throughout history He has consistently called women out from the shadows to be seen and heard by the whole of their community. He is still calling us today.

Faith Discovered

Then he said to her, "Daughter, your faith has healed you. Go in peace." (verse 48)

Just listen to Jesus' wise and healing words. He offered her a new identity: daughter. What other word could have been more loving? Daughter. A word that means intimate, provisional, accepting, tenderly loving relationship. A word that denotes personal relationship and an ongoing commitment to care. Again, in this unique context of Jairus' plea for his daughter's healing, how much richer that title became. Even as Jesus affirmed her self-advocacy, He let her know she was not alone in that effort. He, too, became her advocate, the One who sought her good, her complete healing, even when she could not.

Also, Jesus connected her faith with her healing: "Daughter, your faith has healed you." He highlighted her part in her story of healing and did it with such clarity that she could neither dismiss nor diminish it. He knew that her feminine tendency would not be to diminish *His* part in the process, but *her* part. Jesus wanted her to become more aware of her own resources and choices and their critically important impact on her experience of healing. Naming it so clearly helped her recognize her faith, perhaps for the first time.

Lastly, He said, "Go in peace." We get a sense that the work was finally finished. The peace she left with was a complete and enduring peace. It would last far longer than the wellness of her body. It would bring a kind of restoration far richer than the social and religious inclusion now available to her. The woman with the hemorrhage was now the woman whose faith had made her well, the daughter of the Messiah.

Amazingly, that same healing and life-changing faith are available to you today. What will you choose?

YOUR JOURNEY

For personal reflection and group discussion

1. List five pivotal, fork-in-the-road decisions you have made in your life.

2. List five experiences you now see as missed opportunities.

3. Identify any points of pain, suffering, grief, or loss in your life that you tend to dismiss or diminish. Have you dared to speak for God while running from your pain? Imagine Jesus' attentiveness to all your needs.

4. Review the areas of your life that need God's healing touch. How have those areas of pain and suffering influenced your self-image?

5. Choose one of these areas and describe, in as much detail as possible, what healing might look like in your life. Seek to acknowledge all possible responses, fears, and disruptions in relationships that might accompany such a healing.

6. As best you can, describe what you would be like as a completely whole woman. Hear again Jesus' stubborn commitment to your wholeness.

7. Tell a story of past healing from your life that you have not told publicly before. You may choose to tell either an individual or a group. Dare to experience an even more complete healing.

8. Identify the part faith played in your healing. What choices did you make, large or small?

9. What specific choices can you make this week to move toward healing? What must you let go of in order to move in that direction?

10. What words do you most want to hear from Jesus?

CHAPTER SIX

Hearing God's Promise, Growing Toward God's Call

Sarai in Genesis 12–17

As women focused on nurturing growth in others, we often neglect to listen for our own invitations from God. When we speak of God's founding work of establishing the Jewish nation through promises to Abram, how often do we, like both Sarai and Abram, diminish God's equally momentous promise to Sarai? As we look more closely at Sarai's critically important calling and faith, we can see our own callings in a new, more significant light.

To Consider . . .

Have you ever sensed God calling you to do something? Describe the experience and your response.

"WHOSE cry have you heard?" The speaker's words echoed in the expansive and utterly silent hotel ballroom. He had just finished telling the story of Moses for hundreds of conference attendees. He highlighted Moses' unique life history, having been born a Jew but raised as a prince of Egypt and eventually finding his way back to his people of birth. He also talked about his unique place in the history of the nation of Israel, his calling to lead his people out of bondage in Egypt and into God's Promised Land.

As the speaker walked through the story, he pointed out for us the specifics of that unique call from God. He noted especially that many times in Exodus 3, God said, "I have heard the cry of my people." He observed that though Moses was clearly and specifically qualified for the job, his invitation to join God's work was rooted not in those abilities but instead in the pain of hurting people.

"Whose cry have you heard?" Even as those words penetrated deeper into my being, I instantly knew my answer: wounded women in the church. For many of my thirty-eight years, I had been the recipient of story after story of women whose pain in life had been increased, as well as assuaged, by their spiritual community. I knew from the healing of my own feminine soul in the previous three years that this was never God's intention.

"Whose cry have you heard?" Oddly, I had never thought of those incidents as an indication of my calling. In fact, I had never thought of having a calling at all. As a wife and mother of three school-age kids and an active member in our small church, simply dealing with the needs before me was more than I could handle on most days. Yet there I sat in that well-stuffed, straight-backed hotel chair, not only moved by the question but also having an undeniably clear answer.

Over the next few months, the seed that was planted that day took on a life of its own. Though I had yearned for years for more formal education in the arena of Christian counseling, that dream simply was not practical. The school I was interested in attending was across the country. Now, unexpectedly fueled by the cry of the people, I found myself sending off for a brochure. My husband and I began to talk more seriously and dream together about the possibility of this move.

Our children, ages sixteen, thirteen, and ten, were stunned and understandably alarmed, especially when I pulled out the brochure at dinner one night. The distant possibility became all too real in an instant. They were not the only ones upset.

My actions surprised and alarmed a lot of people in my world, people who loved me and were genuinely concerned for my family and me. What could I be thinking, taking three well-adjusted kids at such critical ages away from their friends and schools and church? Their loving warnings sank deep into my being.

The loudest voices of concern were in my own head. The accusations echoed: *How could you be so selfish? Surely you will regret this. What's your hurry? There will be time for yourself later.* Yet my sense of urgency remained. Somehow, I knew there would never be a "good" time, a convenient time, to answer this calling.

The bottom line remained: The fear of *not* following this new direction was greater than the fear of following. It was not a fear of punishment as much as a fear of stagnation. What would happen to my soul if I ignored this next step? My understanding of God's purpose for my life was admittedly limited and imperfect, but this was all I had. Though quite a leap circumstantially, it seemed like just the next step in my spiritual journey.

My husband, Bob, rode the waves of critique with me, one of the few who knew both the depth and source of my calling. He took great personal and professional risks in support of my vision. As an environmental engineer who worked for a consulting firm, he inquired about the possibility of keeping his job and simply working three thousand miles west of his rather stable clientele. Miraculously, his company agreed to the plan. Yet the sense of calling was mine alone, not his. Though he faithfully shouldered huge portions of the physical and financial burden, most of the emotional weight of this move and the rage of my hurting children were on me. Such struggles were intensified by the fact that this calling came with no guarantees or clarity about what life would look like beyond graduate school. All I knew was this step.

As we prepared to move, Bob and I spent one thousand dollars (a *lot* of money!) on a house-hunting trip to Seattle. The housing market was unimaginably tight. Though we looked feverishly for an entire long weekend, we headed home with only one slim chance of a contract. At a layover stop in Denver, we called our Realtor to discover that even that slim chance had vanished.

In the air once again, I stared blankly into the clouds outside the airplane window, feeling shock, disappointment, despair. The thought of moving our family of five was hard enough. The thought of moving without a home to move to seemed unbearable. Suddenly, the clouds cleared and my eyes focused on the terrain below. Winding back and forth beneath me was the dark blue ribbon of a river. I have always been amazed at how rivers seem to dance as they twist and turn toward the sea. Right next to the river was a road, straight as an arrow, a hard mass of concrete moving from point A to point B with great efficiency and little creativity, imagination, or life.

The words of an old song surfaced from somewhere deep inside my soul: "Can I have this dance for the rest of your life?" I knew instantly that this journey of calling was going to look much more like a lively, winding river than a hard, efficient highway. I could fight and grieve that reality or accept God's lilting invitation and learn to dance in the swirling, life-giving waters of my God's creative and imaginative path. For me, the choice was easy: I love to dance! The image of that moment has remained with me since that time, often offering insight, hope, and comfort. (I call it my one-thousand-dollar image!)

As the path of our move to Seattle unfolded, God provided at every turn. Still, the cost was high on every front: financially, relationally, socially. High, yet doable. My sense of calling was insistent. So we sold our house, and off we went: a family of five, a nine-year-old dachshund, and all our worldly goods in a U-Haul truck. And that was just the beginning of answering God's call on my feminine soul.

AN ANCIENT WOMAN'S SOUL

Along that path, I found yet another faithful ancient mentor: Sarah. Because we will explore so much of her story, we will divide it into two chapters. Sarai, as she was named when we first meet her in Genesis 12–17, is best known to most of us simply as Abram's wife. She is often an almost invisible part in the story of the origins of our faith. Yet if we look again, we can see that though she did indeed begin as an invisible woman, she grew into a woman with a profound sense of calling, personhood, and single-minded obedience to God. As you read her story, note the gradual birthing process of this woman's soul as God gently drew her continually in the direction of a stronger sense of self, voice, and calling.

Almost Invisible

The Lord had said to Abram, "Leave your country, your people and your father's household and go to the land I will show you.

"I will make you into a great nation
    and I will bless you;
I will make your name great,
    and you will be a blessing.
I will bless those who bless you,
    and whoever curses you I will curse;
and all peoples on earth
    will be blessed through you."

So Abram left, as the Lord had told him; and Lot went with him. Abram was seventy-five years old when he set out from Haran. He took his wife Sarai, his nephew Lot, all the possessions they had accumulated and the people they had acquired in Haran, and they set out for the land of Canaan, and they arrived there. (12:1-5)

As the story of the Jews began, God spoke to Abram and invited him into a new and special relationship. Sarai was mentioned as the wife that Abram *took*, along with a nephew, possessions, and acquired people. Not a very flattering first impression but probably an accurate one. Culturally,

88

women of that era had no rights and no standing apart from their husband's will and whim.

The absence of a sense of Sarai's personhood here allows us to see even more clearly in later chapters of Genesis what growth looked like for her as a woman. Even against the grain of this cultural norm, we will see Sarai bloom.

Cultural norms supporting invisibility for women still exist today. For many, hiding their feminine soul is seen as harmless, a neutral cultural choice. Some see it as admirable. Others see it as a simple preference on their part, an election of a legitimate option, a matter of personality. For some it seems to be a vehicle for acquiring much-longed-for security. Yet as Sarai's story unfolds, we see that the choice to hide ourselves is not relationally neutral, and it is definitely not a context in which love will flourish. If we listen well to her story, we will discover that it was never God's intent for Sarai to be known as a silent partner or a nonperson.

Worse Than Invisible

Now there was a famine in the land, and Abram went down to Egypt to live there for a while because the famine was severe. As he was about to enter Egypt, he said to his wife Sarai, "I know what a beautiful woman you are. When the Egyptians see you, they will say, 'This is his wife.' Then they will kill me but will let you live. Say you are my sister, so that I will be treated well for your sake and my life will be spared because of you."

When Abram came to Egypt, the Egyptians saw that she was a very beautiful woman. And when Pharaoh's officials saw her, they praised her to Pharaoh, and she was taken into his palace. He treated Abram well for her sake, and Abram acquired sheep and cattle, male and female donkeys, menservants and maidservants, and camels.

But the Lord inflicted serious diseases on Pharaoh and his household because of Abram's wife Sarai. So Pharaoh summoned Abram. "What have you done to me?" he said. "Why didn't you tell me she was your wife? Why did you say,

'She is my sister,' so that I took her to be my wife? Now then, here is your wife. Take her and go!" Then Pharaoh gave orders about Abram to his men, and they sent him on his way, with his wife and everything he had. (verses 10-20)

Sarai, once simply invisible, was now actively abused. Abram's reasoning was sound and utterly rational. At the same time, the language of this passage, and possibly his motivation, is oriented primarily around his personal concerns. He identified the problem source as Sarai's beauty. He identified the solution as her deception. He identified the desired outcome as good treatment for himself. There is a notable absence of any concern for her treatment, her integrity, or her life experience. There is no record of anything *she* said or did. In fact, when the king was raging at Abram, he even credited Abram, not Sarai as had been planned, with the intentionally deceitful information that she was his sister.

Invisibility is a context for abuse. To the degree that we choose to hide our feminine souls, we foster an environment in which abuse can flourish. *Though we are never responsible for an abuser's unloving choice*, it is critical to recognize the part we play in the abuser/victim cycle. For many of us, the experience of being another's pawn is all it takes to convince us of our need to become more aware of our dignity and personhood. Sarai seems to have learned from this degrading and frightening experience. We see in the next passage that she had learned to speak, albeit not yet with much wisdom.

A False Conclusion, an Abandoned Hope

Now Sarai, Abram's wife, had borne him no children. But she had an Egyptian maidservant named Hagar; so she said to Abram, "The Lord has kept me from having children. Go, sleep with my maidservant; perhaps I can build a family through her." (16:1-2)

As humans, it is unavoidable to try to make sense out of our suffering. Recently I helped employees at a local business try to make some sense of their coworker's suicide. Though ultimately much of our conjecture in such moments will forever remain unconfirmed, conclusions (even false ones) offer us comfort in the midst of pain.

Such was Sarai's conclusion that the Lord had kept her from having children. We know little about Sarai's relationship with God at this point. Because Abram's relationship with God was so centered in previous promises (see 12:1-5), we assume the same was true for Sarai. Though at first those promises had held hope and vision, years of infertility had turned them into painful disappointment.

Enduring years of unfulfilled desire had gotten old. Sarai was ready for resolution, one way or the other. So she opted out of the struggle by concluding that it was not God's will for her to have children. She abandoned her greatest hope and settled for less, offering up Hagar as a substitute by which God could fulfill His promise to the Jewish nation.

How often have we as women in the church done the same thing? How often have we, having been excluded from decision making, concluded that God never intended for us to have a voice? How easily have we given up our place because the road was longer or more difficult than we had anticipated? Often the most powerful objection to our inclusion as women, though not always the most obvious one, comes from within us.

When planning a coed retreat recently, I was not surprised by the request that the small groups be divided by gender. A woman who knew her community well said, "If you put the women in with the men, they won't talk." How often I've spoken with women in touch with needs within their church but unwilling to work through or with the men of the community to most effectively meet those needs. In many ways, we have opted out of the church as a whole, passively participating in dividing the church in ways God never intended.

At times our exclusion from God's work is as real as Sarai's infertility. In those times it is far easier to draw false conclusions, to blame, and to settle for less than it is to persevere in our vision, struggle, and unfulfilled desire. It is critically important to own that we, like Sarai, have sometimes been the *first* ones to give up the vision of our contribution to the whole of the church, unwilling to remain engaged in the difficult and painful struggle.

An Awkward Beginning

Abram agreed to what Sarai said. So after Abram had been living in Canaan ten years, Sarai his wife took her Egyptian maidservant Hagar and gave her to her husband to be his wife. He slept with Hagar, and she conceived.

When she knew she was pregnant, she began to despise her mistress. Then Sarai said to Abram, "You are responsible for the wrong I am suffering. I put my servant in your arms, and now that she knows she is pregnant, she despises me. May the Lord judge between you and me."

"Your servant is in your hands," Abram said. "Do with her whatever you think best." Then Sarai mistreated Hagar; so she fled from her. (verses 2-6)

As we have noted in other chapters, when we begin to grow beyond our tendency to hide, our first steps are often awkward. It is difficult to grow into self-awareness and voice, and Sarai was no exception. Though her fumbling initiative has been viewed in many ways, from a clear example of a manipulative and accusing woman to the cause of present-day conflict in the Middle East, I believe that's not all there is to be seen in this story. The first time Sarai spoke, her first words were, "The LORD" (see verses 1-2). God was clearly a part of her life. She spoke about what she desperately wanted: a family. She also had a plan: Hagar. When the plan backfired, again she was not silent. Though it is difficult for us to understand her justification, somehow she felt that God would be her defender. After all, God had protected her in Egypt.

To say the least, her recruitment and subsequent abuse of Hagar were not her finest moments. Her immaturity and sinful choices are evident. Her life was also full of understandable anger, possibly rooted in the pain of her infertility, Abram's previous abandonment of her, and her perception that God had denied her heart's greatest desire. As we sometimes do, she took that anger out on the nearest available targets: Hagar and Abram.

As Sarai began to own her personhood, both the good and the bad were revealed. Movement out of hiding inevitably uncovers *all* of who we are. For many, the first emotion to surface is anger. Though I do not celebrate or glorify Sarai's unloving behavior, I do applaud her first steps away from invisibility. This was her unique (and awkward) passage into greater growth and maturity.

God's Dual Invitation

When Abram was ninety-nine years old, the Lord appeared to him and said, "I am God Almighty; walk before me and be blameless. I will confirm my covenant between me and you and will greatly increase your numbers."

Abram fell facedown, and God said to him, "As for me, this is my covenant with you: You will be the father of many nations. No longer will you be called Abram; your name will be Abraham, for I have made you a father of many nations. I will make you very fruitful; I will make nations of you, and kings will come from you. I will establish my covenant as an everlasting covenant between me and you and your descendants after you for the generations to come, to be your God and the God of your descendants after you. The whole land of Canaan, where you are now an alien, I will give as an everlasting possession to you and your descendants after you; and I will be their God."

Then God said to Abraham, "As for you, you must keep my covenant, you and your descendants after you for the generations to come. This is my covenant with you and your descendants after you, the covenant you are to keep: Every male among you shall be circumcised. You are to undergo circumcision, and it will be the sign of the covenant between me and you. For the generations to come every male among you who is eight days old must be circumcised, including those born in your household or bought with money from a foreigner—those who are not your offspring. Whether born in your household or bought with your money, they must be circumcised. My covenant in your flesh is to be an everlasting covenant. Any uncircumcised male, who has not been circumcised in the flesh, will be cut off from his people; he has broken my covenant."

God also said to Abraham, "As for Sarai your wife, you are no longer to call her Sarai; her name will be Sarah. I will bless her and will surely give you a son by her. I will bless her so that she will be the mother of nations; kings of peoples will come from her." (17:1-16)

When God made this promise to Sarai, He was not blind to the events of chapter 16. Sarai was not perfect, but she was chosen—invited to be a part of God's plan to grow a nation. Even as she spoke for the first time, God addressed her specifically for the first time. God made it abundantly clear that this long-awaited child of promise would be *her* son, too. She, too, was renamed. She, too, was blessed.

God preserved Sarai's place in the promise in the midst of her lost hope and vision. God has also done the same for us as women in the church who struggle even now to find our place in God's story. God saw the need for the nation to have a mother as well as a father. Though clearly Sarai's and Abram's roles were different, there was equality in the essential language in this passage: the renaming, the blessing, the envisioning of a future. This moment echoes back to Creation when God created both male and female in His image. It is very significant that as God inaugurated this new covenant, this new approach to relationship with humankind, both genders were again specifically and equally included. God appears intent on maximizing both difference and equality.

How sad that we in the church have missed God's vision for the greater glory of both the mother and father of God's chosen people. Beyond physical childbirth, we seldom hear much of what Sarai did to mother this seedling of a nation. As Abram demonstrates next, for some reason the critical importance of the equality of this moment has been especially difficult to grasp, even from the very beginning.

A Lesser Vision

Abraham fell facedown; he laughed and said to himself, "Will a son be born to a man a hundred years old? Will Sarah bear a child at the age of ninety?" And Abraham said to God, "If only Ishmael might live under your blessing!" (verses 17-18)

Though Abraham did not laugh right in God's face, he sure came close. Most of us know about Sarah's response of laughter when she first heard this news (addressed in chapter 7 of this book), but little is said of Abraham's laughter.

It is not hard to see where Abraham was coming from. Relationally, adding another son to the already potentially explosive mix of these two women in his household would be disastrous. He had thirteen years invested in one son, in one understanding of what the fulfillment of God's promise would look like. Fundamentally, if Sarah's inclusion meant this much disruption, he would just as soon leave her out. And so began, I believe, a long tradition of struggle. I readily acknowledge that God's choice of a dual promise, with men *and* women equally important in God's work, is a very messy proposition. It adds tension, complications, and inefficiencies. Men and women alike often resist the idea. It seems foolish, sometimes even laughable. Yet surprisingly, in God's eyes it also seems to be nonnegotiable.

God's "Yes, But . . ."

Then God said, "Yes, but your wife Sarah will bear you a son, and you will call him Isaac. I will establish my covenant with him as an everlasting covenant for his descendants after him. And as for Ishmael, I have heard you: I will surely bless him; I will make him fruitful and will greatly increase his numbers. He will be the father of twelve rulers, and I will make him into a great nation. But my covenant I will establish with Isaac, whom Sarah will bear to you by this time next year." When he had finished speaking with Abraham, God went up from him. (verses 19-22)

God's affirmation of His dual invitation to relationship and ministry was anything but vague. He began and ended this section with undeniably clear language. Sandwiched between, however, God's heart of compassion came through. Abraham was in a rough spot. He had genuine concern for the only son he had known, the son he thought was the promised child. God lovingly and specifically reassured Abraham that Ishmael, too, would be blessed.

As women, we can hear this affirmation of Sarah's unquestionable part in God's plan as God's invitation to us today. Many of us, as was true for myself, are so caught up in the nurturing and urgent duties of the day that we fail to even ask the questions necessary to discern God's calling for us in the larger scope of kingdom work. From the tone of this passage, it seems God has bigger plans for us than we often dare to imagine. Listen well, oh Sarais of the church: God is calling your name.

YOUR JOURNEY

For personal reflection and group discussion

1. List five situations that break your heart.

2. List five encounters with others that have made you so angry you could spit.

3. Whose cry have you heard? Reexamine those things that make you angry or break your heart, because they can often give you clues to discern your calling.

4. Where are you currently in regard to the idea of being called by God? Oblivious? Too busy? Doubting your suitability? Unsure of your passions?

5. Have there been times in your life when your choice to hide allowed others to take advantage of you? Has anyone in your life "sold you out"? If so, describe the situation.

6. Are there previous callings you have lost hope for or abandoned or things you've attempted but felt you failed to accomplish? Have you in some way found a substitute or handed over your personal vision to another?

7. How do you see men and women with respect to the work of God? What is the same for both sexes? What is different? Do you see both genders as equally critical to kingdom work?

8. Describe a circumstance when you felt excluded from a part of God's work because of your gender. How did you feel?

9. How understanding are you of your learning curve as you seek to grow?

CHAPTER SEVEN

Living God's Call,
Growing in Groundedness and Confidence

Sarah in Genesis 17–23

As Sarah began to live out God's calling in her life, she encountered deep joy and uniquely feminine challenges. Struggling against relational forces from within and without, she became ever more confident and grounded in the importance of her calling as the mother of God's promise.

To Consider . . .

List three long-standing but unfulfilled dreams. Why haven't they come true for you?

I CAN best describe my year in graduate school as a season of blooming. I felt more alive and beautiful than I could ever remember feeling. I was fed, nurtured, challenged, cared for, affirmed, listened to, taught, drawn out, celebrated, and encouraged in ways that changed me forever. It was a real natural high, which was followed, as you might imagine, by a very different kind of season. This journey of answering my calling was definitely going to look more like navigating a twisting, turning river than driving down an efficiently designed highway.

Because the cost of living in Seattle was high, our family of five could survive financially as we were for only a year. Once again, just as I had done when we decided to move away from Texas, I began to negotiate my *ideas* about my calling to minister to wounded women with the *reality* of all my other callings in life. It was usually hard to determine whether I was wisely negotiating or unwisely compromising. In considering our options, the rest of the family outvoted me, and soon we were on our way back to Texas. My few remaining courses would be completed long-distance. For me, it was a trail of many tears.

Even through those tears, I somehow knew that this, too, was a part of my calling. No matter what it felt like, I knew that God had not brought me back to Texas to kill off my vision and momentum. During the next year, completing my degree and getting our household settled again took all my attention. Along the way, God provided both comfort and surprising resources for continued growth.

One thing that God chose not to provide, however, was clarity on the next step in my journey toward fully living my calling. Even a year after graduation, I had little idea of what I was to do with my new degree or how I was to use it to help others. Though God continued to bring hurting women across my path, "doing lunch really well" just did not seem like enough. None of my previous ideas about how my life might look at this point came to fruition. Internally, self-doubt was a continual challenge. Had I been mistaken or simply foolish? It felt as if I were going nowhere fast on this circuitous river ride.

As our son prepared to go off to college, I prepared to find a job—any job—to help pay for his tuition and room and board. Once again, the question of wise negotiation or unwise compromise surfaced for me. There was precious little certainty to comfort me. After weeks of looking, my first job offer came as a very unexpected bend in the river. I was actually interviewing for a different job at a local hospital when I was offered the position of staff chaplain by a delightful and wise Irish Catholic sister, Sister Marian. She was a visionary woman. While my training and experience had prepared me well for the job, I had never even considered chaplaincy. Despite my surprise, I could see God's fingerprints of grace all over this opportunity.

Though I was deeply thankful for the job, working full-time was a huge and very painful adjustment for me. I felt as if I had been knocked off my center, exiled to a foreign land. My encounter with the significant grief of this change was an unexpected challenge from within. When friends asked me excitedly if I liked my new job, I had no idea what to say. Few seemed to understand my deep sense of loss. So many points of pleasure and satisfaction during my years at home were no longer part of my life: a carefully prepared meal, a clean house, hours of time alone, gardening, baking cookies with the kids (even teenagers!). I missed my old life tremendously.

At the same time, all I was learning in this new world intrigued me. With wise and continual support from coworkers, I found deep satisfaction in companioning people through some of the most painful moments of their lives. As Sister Marian graciously mentored me, she was careful to emphasize the need for me to do my job as only I could, expressing the uniqueness of my feminine soul.

Again, I encountered an unexpected challenge. The chaplain assigned to the intensive care unit prior to me was male. As the new kid on the block, I was very tempted to try to walk in his shoes, doing the job just as he had. The ICU staff had understandable preconceptions of how the job should be done. I struggled to resist the pull of those preexisting expectations as I found my own feminine ways of offering comfort and spiritual nurture.

Daily, I felt myself growing stronger and more confident. Even in the midst of an exhausting job, I could sense within myself new capacities for love and endurance. Often finding myself in utterly overwhelming situations, I learned to trust my gut, to trust the goodness that many years of knowing Jesus had woven into the fabric of my soul. With each new encounter, I became more aware of what a difference I could make in this new world of mine. For me, offering a more feminine brand of healing compassion meant using fewer words, more emotion, less movement, more stillness, fewer agendas, and more focus on being a calm, compassionate presence in the midst of whatever the moment might hold. I was encouraged to find that offering others the best of what God had placed within me brought real comfort to people in pain.

As a woman ministering in the Bible belt, I had my share of gender-related challenges, too. I will never forget the day Mr. Carter, a man with staunchly conservative roots, took me aside and tearfully thanked me for the help and comfort I had offered him in his brother's month-long journey toward death following a tragic car accident. He confessed that the first day I walked in and introduced myself as the ICU chaplain, he had completely dismissed the possibility that I could help him in any way. Yet day after day as I listened, affirmed, prayed, wept, and mostly just stood with him in silence at his brother's bedside, God had brought comfort. Mr. Carter was unwilling to ignore the reality of that comfort, even if it did not fit his initial expectations or usual categories. When I attended his brother's funeral, he even invited me to sit with the family. Amazing grace.

Thankful for my new sense of confidence and effectiveness, I was also curious about the other challenging opportunities that came my way simply because I now had a job title: chaplain. Though that title had not imparted any wisdom that I had not previously possessed, somehow it offered a sense of status that many in the world equate with wisdom. I was invited to speak at churches and lead training workshops. I began to appreciate the good that could be accomplished within the bowels of seemingly cold corporate systems.

In those years of working full-time in the hospital, my sense of being drawn toward hurting women in particular never left me. I lived many amazing moments with women there, some reflected in this book. Three years later, the season changed once again as I left my job at the hospital.

While the circumstances shifted around me, my calling became clearer and more grounded within me.

As one season ebbed, another began to flow. In addition to being stronger and more confident, I had also learned a thing or two about negotiating my calling through the challenge of shifting seasons. Home full-time once again, I was curious about when and where and how my unique assignment from God would surface. Learning to ride the river well, I was definitely expecting another surprise.

Sure enough, it came. Seemingly from out of nowhere, I rediscovered a long-neglected passion for writing. With the help of my husband and three children, I converted half our attic space to a study, complete with serenely gentle turquoise-colored walls; a soft, white wool rug; and a Gaiam BalanceBall chair. Though the day-to-day experience of living my calling had taken on a whole new look, once again I heard God's invitation to pursue with renewed vigor my ministry to women.

AN ANCIENT WOMAN'S SOUL

When we left our story in the middle of Genesis 17, Abraham had just received the commandment for circumcision and new, more specific promises for both him and his newly named wife, Sarah. As we will see in Genesis 17–23, some of God's revealed plans were easier to comply with than others.

Inaction Exposed

On that very day Abraham took his son Ishmael and all those born in his household or bought with his money, every male in his household, and circumcised them, as God told him. Abraham was ninety-nine years old when he was circumcised, and his son Ishmael was thirteen; Abraham and his son Ishmael were both circumcised on that same day. And every male in Abraham's household, including those born in his household or bought from a foreigner, was circumcised with him.

The Lord appeared to Abraham near the great trees of Mamre while he was sitting at the entrance to his tent in the heat of the day. Abraham looked up and saw three men standing nearby. When he saw them, he hurried from the entrance of his tent to meet them and bowed low to the ground.

He said, "If I have found favor in your eyes, my lord, do not pass your servant by. Let a little water be brought, and then you may all wash your feet and rest under this tree. Let me get you something to eat, so you can be refreshed and then go on your way—now that you have come to your servant."

"Very well," they answered, "do as you say."

So Abraham hurried into the tent to Sarah. "Quick," he said, "get three seahs of fine flour and knead it and bake some bread."

Then he ran to the herd and selected a choice, tender calf and gave it to a servant, who hurried to prepare it. He then brought some curds and milk and the calf that had been prepared, and set these before them. While they ate, he stood near them under a tree.

"Where is your wife Sarah?" they asked him.

"There, in the tent," he said.

Then the Lord said, "I will surely return to you about this time next year, and Sarah your wife will have a son."

Now Sarah was listening at the entrance to the tent, which was behind him. Abraham and Sarah were already old and well advanced in years, and Sarah was past the age of childbearing. So Sarah laughed to herself as she thought, "After I am worn out and my master is old, will I now have this pleasure?"

Then the Lord said to Abraham, "Why did Sarah laugh and say, 'Will I really have a child, now that I am old?' Is anything too hard for the Lord? I will return to you at the appointed time next year and Sarah will have a son." (17:23–18:14)

The story of the three angel visitors in Genesis 18 is an oft-told story in our Christian tradition, generally seen as a shining example of hospitality or a reiteration of God's promise to Abraham. I invite you to look at it a bit differently. Perhaps it is not so much about informing Abraham but rather exposing Abraham's lack of action regarding his part in fulfilling the promises of God and informing Sarah.

In Genesis 17, Abraham was clearly told that Sarah would have a son. He was also given the commandment for circumcision, which he faithfully and immediately obeyed. We do not know precisely what the time gap was between chapters 17 and 18, but this we can infer: It was long enough for a circumcision to heal, as evidenced by the fact that Abraham was running around as he offered hospitality to these holy strangers.

So with the promise given and the wound healed, one might naturally assume that Abraham, even at the age of one hundred, had begun to act on the promises of God—act sexually, that is. The next logical step toward obedience would be to approach Sarah. The writer makes it clear that Abraham was able enough for the task at hand. Able, but maybe not yet willing.

Enter the visitors. It is notable that their conversation began with an inquiry about Sarah, possibly a clue as to the reason for their visit. One visitor, the Lord, then repeated the exact words that had been spoken to Abraham previously in chapter 17. This was not new news to Abraham, but it was to Sarah, as indicated by her response of surprised laughter. Perhaps her incredulity was more a response to Abraham's lack of communication and obedience than it was evidence of her lack of faith.

Her carefully recorded but unspoken words further expose his avoidance: "After I am worn out and my master is old, will I now have this pleasure?" The word translated here as *pleasure* literally means "delight"; this is the only time this particular word is used in the Bible. Though it could be referencing the future child, some scholars believe it is speaking about the act of sexual intercourse.[1] We might, therefore, conclude that Abraham had not yet even approached Sarah sexually.

Into that context of circumstantial exposure, the all-knowing Lord directly raised the rhetorical question to Abraham: "Why did Sarah laugh?" In other words, "Why is this news to her?" The Lord then reminded *Abraham*, not Sarah, that nothing is too hard for God. The word for *hard* can be translated as "marvelous" or "extraordinary." Maybe what stalled Abraham was not so much rebellion but the familiar flagging of hope. After years of trying and waiting for a child with his beloved Sarai, it may have felt too painful to engage that specific desire once again. Maybe the news was just too good to be true. But whatever his reason, Sarah's part in this promise was no longer Abraham's secret.

Acting as Sarah's advocate, God preserved her role in the promise even in the midst of Abraham's failure to accept it. As we noted in the previous chapter, God had preserved Sarai's part when even she could not see it. Recall that Sarai sought to relinquish her role by giving Hagar to Abram.

We all, both men and women, often dismiss the critically important dual nature of our faith community. At times, we women have sold ourselves short, being content to remain in the safety of the shadows. At other times, women in the church have met such resistance that they have wondered if they were fighting God Himself for a part in kingdom work. This foundational story of faith powerfully counters the belief that a woman's equal role in our communities is optional. Let us be assured that God never intended for women to be excluded from an equal and essential part in His work on earth. What human frailty sometimes fails to see, God does not.

This reading of this passage is new thinking for many. Yet given Abraham's initial reluctance to accept Sarah's inclusion in the promise (see Genesis 17), it is not a stretch. For many women who have felt shut out of kingdom work, in large or small ways, this story can be immensely healing. You are not alone. And you are not without an Advocate.

An Invitation to Honesty

Sarah was afraid, so she lied and said, "I did not laugh." But he said, "Yes, you did laugh." (18:15)

Lest we think Abraham is the only one in this story to suffer from human frailty, the writer immediately reveals one of Sarah's core struggles. As already mentioned, men and women may sin differently, but we all struggle with sin. Read through an exclusively masculine lens for far too long, our more feminine struggles have often been sadly misunderstood.

This moment in Sarah's story is a good example. It is often taught that Sarah's sin was to laugh, supposing a lack of faith. Some believe the angel was rebuking her for this. But there might be another way to see this part of the conversation.

The text specifically says that Sarah was afraid. Whom might Sarah have feared? Clearly she heard the conversation the Lord had just had with Abraham, and there was probably a tone of rebuke in His voice. Her husband was in trouble because the divine guest had been offended, and the offense was now connected to her laughter. She had no way of knowing the real cause of the offense (Abraham's delayed obedience); all she knew was that her laughter had prompted this divine guest's confrontational response.

For most women, it is very uncomfortable to be the source of exposure or trouble for another person, no matter how innocently we may come into that role. Sarah sought to undo the problem she felt she had caused. She tried to save her husband from God Himself. In her attempt to become her husband's savior, rescuer, and caretaker at all costs, she ended up a liar, compromising her personal integrity.

I hear in the Lord's response to her a simple invitation to dare to live honestly despite the situation with her husband, whatever the painful consequences might have been for those she loved. How often do we as women cover for people we love and call it godly? How often do we use untold amounts of energy trying to compensate for their lack of care and call it nurturing? Some in churches today teach that such compensation is our feminine calling—that we should give 200 percent, especially in marriage relationships. Some even say this is what it means to respect one's husband: to cover his frailties, disobedience, or even abuse.

God knows our feminine liabilities, our sinful tendencies, and our unhealthy extremes. I believe that God is inviting us all, through Sarah, to envision a new kind of respect. Might it be that truly respecting the men around us, including our husbands, means expecting the greatest good from their lives and gently refusing to settle for anything less? Could our habit of lowering expectations, compensating, and covering for them be, in fact, an act of rank *disrespect*? Maybe our motivation for protecting them is more about protecting ourselves from pain and disappointment than about loving our husbands. Certainly God's love for all of us continually invites us to be more closely the people God created us to be. That includes uncomfortable moments. Why would our love reflect anything less? Why would we lie to get someone else out of trouble? Why would we cover or deflect blame onto ourselves?

Again, though for men, maturity might come in the form of increased sensitivity to those around them and reduced self-awareness, that is not the direction of the growth pictured here for Sarah. Instead, God was asking of her a willingness to be honest no matter what the consequence. Generally speaking, we as women struggle to ground ourselves in truth as all our various sensitivities to relationship swirl around us. We must learn not to fear the truth, to be confident and bold in our honest response.

It is debatable as to whether Sarah's laughter was sin or not. Some say it was lack of faith,[2] some immature doubt, others a momentary reaction of surprise that was not reflective of her faith at all. Less open to debate is the sinfulness of her attempt to cover and undo her honest response. Through her story, we can hear the voice of the Lord saying to us, "It's okay to be honest about your relationships, even if your honesty creates some trouble for another." Does that mean we have a biblical mandate to "air our dirty laundry" for all to see? Clearly no. But neither are we to pretend. Our invitation is to respond honestly to relationships and situations around us, refusing the temptation to lie or hide the truth out of fear.

The Lord offered Sarah the freedom to live her honest response to life. Having defended her part in the promise here, God knew this would not be her last challenge. Sarah needed to learn to face each threat with courage and personal integrity, not innocence and naïveté, and to ground herself in her calling rather than in the fear of displeasing others. Sarah would mature only through facing and overcoming these uniquely feminine challenges.

Three Steps Forward, Two Steps Back

Now Abraham moved on from there into the region of the Negev and lived between Kadesh and Shur. For a while he stayed in Gerar, and there Abraham said of his wife Sarah, "She is my sister." Then Abimelech king of Gerar sent for Sarah and took her.

But God came to Abimelech in a dream one night and said to him, "You are as good as dead because of the woman you have taken; she is a married woman."

Now Abimelech had not gone near her, so he said, "Lord, will you destroy an innocent nation? Did he not say to me, 'She is my sister,' and didn't she also say, 'He is my brother'? I have done this with a clear conscience and clean hands."

Then God said to him in the dream, "Yes, I know you did this with a clear conscience, and so I have kept you from sinning against me. That is why I did not let you touch her. Now return the man's wife, for he is a prophet, and he will pray for you and you will live. But if you do not return her, you may be sure that you and all yours will die."

Early the next morning Abimelech summoned all his officials, and when he told them all that had happened, they were very much afraid. Then Abimelech called Abraham in and said, "What have you done to us? How have I wronged you that you have brought such great guilt upon me and my kingdom? You have done things to me that should not be done." And Abimelech asked Abraham, "What was your reason for doing this?"

Abraham replied, "I said to myself, 'There is surely no fear of God in this place, and they will kill me because of my wife.' Besides, she really is my sister, the daughter of my father though not of my mother; and she became my wife. And when God had me wander from my father's household, I said to her, 'This is how you can show your love to me: Everywhere we go, say of me, "He is my brother."'"

Then Abimelech brought sheep and cattle and male and female slaves and gave them to Abraham, and he returned Sarah his wife to him. And Abimelech said, "My land is before you; live wherever you like."

To Sarah he said, "I am giving your brother a thousand shekels of silver. This is to cover the offense against you before all who are with you; you are completely vindicated."

Then Abraham prayed to God, and God healed Abimelech, his wife and his slave girls so they could have children again, for the Lord had closed up every womb in Abimelech's household because of Abraham's wife Sarah. (20:1-18)

This story is very similar to the previous story we explored in Genesis 12. Its inclusion here speaks of a very real life struggle: Old patterns die hard. Abraham moved to the edge of the Promised Land, toward Egypt. The use of symbols in Scripture is generally thought to indicate a move in that direction to be movement away from God. In a tough spot for the second time, Abraham opted for deception. For the second time, Sarah was silent.

In Abraham's public account of his reasoning, he offered a bit of insight into his relationship with Sarah. In seeking her compliance with his plan, he used the ultimate trump card: "This is how you can show your love to me." In some circumstances, those words could be an honest attempt at open and helpful communication. Sometimes we need help understanding how others can best receive our love. Given this context, however, I doubt that was the case here.

Consider what Abraham was asking of Sarah: active deception producing a level of personal vulnerability that could easily have resulted in her rape or death. From our objective distance, it is not difficult to see his approach as a manipulative ploy, undoubtedly motivated by understandable and genuine fear.

Though those we love may not ask us to lie to foreign kings, many women find it nearly impossible to refuse similar messages. Our "This is how you can show your love to me" messages can look like sex on demand in the midst of exhaustion, holidays with the extended family when we long to be home with just our own household, or taking a new high-pressure job to meet someone else's financial goals. As relationally focused women who are eager to express our love for others, we are particularly vulnerable to these less than noble forms of persuasion. Such relational ploys have a way of quickly shutting down appropriate personal caution and healthy self-concern in many women.

Again, how miraculous and healing to see these painful and destructive relational dynamics spelled out in such an ancient text! We often face these same challenges to our growth as women, some birthed from within us, some from without. When we see ourselves on these pages, we know not only that we are known but also that there is hope.

We know that just as God was with Sarah, God is with us, growing us through it all.

Laughter Received

> *Now the Lord was gracious to Sarah as he had said, and the Lord did for Sarah what he had promised. Sarah became pregnant and bore a son to Abraham in his old age, at the very time God had promised him. Abraham gave the name Isaac to the son Sarah bore him. When his son Isaac was eight days old, Abraham circumcised him, as God commanded him. Abraham was a hundred years old when his son Isaac was born to him.*
>
> *Sarah said, "God has brought me laughter, and everyone who hears about this will laugh with me." And she added, "Who would have said to Abraham that Sarah would nurse children? Yet I have borne him a son in his old age." (21:1-7)*

Just as sadness creates a tension within us that cries for release, so, too, does joy. Both extremes also produce a greater personal vulnerability with their expression. Sarah responded to this dream fulfilled with passionate celebration. There was no hint of caution or hesitancy in this happy moment—only sheer delight, a delight she wanted to share with all who cared to listen.

Notice her language. She saw Isaac as a gift from God. She saw this miraculous birth as a community experience and invited everyone to join in her celebrating. Her voice was confident and broadly cast. She remained amazed. As the angel had said, "Is anything too hard for the LORD?"

Sarah had lost hope for this kind of moment with Abraham. Her biggest reason for celebration was the fact that she could offer this amazing gift to her husband and companion of so many years. This special joy revealed her tender and devoted heart of affection for Abraham. In the midst of all the ups and downs, the ins and outs, the general mess and pain of life together, she clearly loved him.

Motherly Protection

The child grew and was weaned, and on the day Isaac was weaned Abraham held a great feast. But Sarah saw that the son whom Hagar the Egyptian had borne to Abraham was mocking, and she said to Abraham, "Get rid of that slave woman and her son, for that slave woman's son will never share in the inheritance with my son Isaac."

The matter distressed Abraham greatly because it concerned his son. But God said to him, "Do not be so distressed about the boy and your maidservant. Listen to whatever Sarah tells you, because it is through Isaac that your offspring will be reckoned. I will make the son of the maidservant into a nation also, because he is your offspring." (21:8-13)

Unlike in fairy tales, the family in this story did not live happily ever after. Though at times tension can be healthy in families, the tension Sarah saw developing between Ishmael and Isaac was not. Note the reason she offered for ousting Hagar and Ishmael: "That slave woman's son will never share in the inheritance with my son Isaac." Sarah felt that God's promise was being challenged. Understanding the significance of that promise for her and Abraham, she knew that Isaac was just the beginning, the seed of something much larger.

Many women have a tough time relating to the idea of being a warrior—that is, with the exception of fighting to protect their children. Some call it the "mother bear syndrome." Sarah's words were not polite or gentle; she literally commanded Abraham to cast out his older son. Her position seems to have been completely void of compassion, especially in contrast to Abraham's.

It is difficult to know how to interpret that absence of compassion on Sarah's part. Could it be that Abraham had told her of God's promise to care for Ishmael (see 17:20) and she was counting on God to intervene and protect elsewhere? Might Sarah's initial bitterness toward Hagar have been unresolved even many years later? No mention is made of God's displeasure at her stern approach; the silence of the text leaves us wondering.

What we can say is that Sarah was acting protectively toward Isaac and guarding the promise. It seems she alone saw this situation as dangerous. Often we as women read relational dynamics differently than men do, seeing potential dangers they would miss. Sarah had learned her lesson from her previous experiences. Grounded in the promise and her calling, she was willing to see reality with honest eyes and confidently confront her husband when necessary. She now held tight to the very promise she herself had once abandoned.

Abraham, however, was struggling. Though God had previously reassured him that He would bless Ishmael as well as Isaac, that promise was a lot easier to trust as long as Ishmael was close by. It is difficult to fault Abraham for his genuine and noble concern for these two human beings, Hagar and Ishmael, regardless of how their lives happened to intersect with God's larger purposes. God did not rebuke Abraham for his concern. Instead, once again, He expressed compassion toward him. Yet in the midst of that compassion, He remained unmoved and clear about the choice.

God told Abraham to "listen to whatever Sarah tells you." Whoa! God expressed great faith in Sarah's wisdom, in her understanding of the plan and work of God. He recognized and affirmed Sarah as the guardian of the promise, a promise that needed a mother's protective love.

For a variety of reasons, women have often been branded as untrustworthy in regard to the work of God. Though we cannot address all the reasons here, suffice it to say that this text, at the very least, offers a clear message endorsing the critical need for the inclusion of the feminine perspective in kingdom decisions.

Planted in the Place of Promise

Sarah lived to be a hundred and twenty-seven years old. She died at Kiriath Arba (that is, Hebron) in the land of Canaan, and Abraham went to mourn for Sarah and to weep over her.

Then Abraham rose from beside his dead wife and spoke to the Hittites. He said, "I am an alien and a stranger among you.

112

Sell me some property for a burial site here so I can bury my dead." . . .

Abraham agreed to Ephron's terms and weighed out for him the price he had named in the hearing of the Hittites: four hundred shekels of silver, according to the weight current among the merchants.

So Ephron's field in Machpelah near Mamre—both the field and the cave in it, and all the trees within the borders of the field—was deeded to Abraham as his property in the presence of all the Hittites who had come to the gate of the city. Afterward Abraham buried his wife Sarah in the cave in the field of Machpelah near Mamre (which is at Hebron) in the land of Canaan. So the field and the cave in it were deeded to Abraham by the Hittites as a burial site. (23:1-4,16-20)

We are not certain where Abraham was living at the time of Sarah's death. The last word recorded (in 22:19) was that he lived in Beersheba at the edge of the Promised Land, spending time in Philistia. Might he and Sarah have been living in different locations? Beersheba was closer to where Hagar and Ishmael lived. Could Abraham still have been struggling to let go of his first son?

In any event, we know Sarah was in Hebron, near the oaks of Mamre, when she died. She planted herself not on the edge but in the center of God's Land of Promise in a place historically connected to the promises of God. Hebron was Sarah's first home in the Promised Land after Abraham and Lot divided the land (see 13:18). It was also the place where the trio of angels visited, informing her for the first time of her specific and personal calling from God (see chapter 18). Such connections are not happenstance. As women, we often use environment—location, home, personal appearance, and so forth—to communicate much about ourselves.

It is sad for me to think that Sarah's choice to ground herself in the heart of this land might have meant that she and Abraham were living apart in their final days. From listening to the stories of many women, I have observed that such a separation of lives, physical or otherwise, is not rare, though it is not commonly acknowledged by many in the church. Relationships often require difficult renegotiation when transforming growth and change occur. It is another messy and painful part of the maturing process for both men and women. Note, however, that it does not necessarily mean a loss of love or commitment. We have no reason to believe that Sarah's sentiments highlighted earlier had changed. Also, in the midst of this possible separation, the fact that Abraham mourned her death makes it clear that he continued to care deeply for Sarah.

Though Abraham had lived in some part of the Land of Promise for years, we are unsure why he had not previously bought any of the land God promised him. It is interesting that it was Sarah's death that prompted his first purchase. Even in her death, the powerful promises of God were still at work through her.

The visual details of this passage intrigue me. In verse 17, we note that all the trees were included in the deeding of the land. In verse 19, the NASB translation notes that the cave Sarah was buried in faced Mamre, the place always connected with those trees. Can you see it? What a beautiful spot, both physically and symbolically—a fitting reward for such a faithful guardian of God's promises. Sarah was the first permanent Jewish resident of the Promised Land.

In reviewing Sarah's story of calling, growth, and faith, it is easy to see why God felt the nation of Israel needed a mother. As she nurtured this nation from promise into reality, God gently drew her out of hiding toward feminine maturity, shaping her into a strong, wise, confident, and memorable matriarch. She was a significant part of the Jewish nation's successful birth with her influence extending far beyond the moment she brought forth Isaac. She heard God's ever-expanding invitation and responded with ever-growing faithfulness.

Sarah's calling was just the beginning. God still has important work for each of us as women today, work that we are uniquely designed to offer. God's kingdom still needs our motherly ways. Sarah's story has inspired and mentored me as I have followed all the twists and turns of God's call on my life. Will you, like Sarah, dare to listen for and follow God's personal calling on your life today?

YOUR JOURNEY

For personal reflection and group discussion

1. When has your honest response created trouble for another? How did you feel? What did you do?

2. When have you found yourself trying to cover or compensate for another at the expense of being honest? Do you see that choice any differently in the light of Sarah's story?

3. What old patterns in your life draw you back into hiding, away from living out your calling?

4. What "This is how you can show your love to me" messages have you received? To what degree were they honest or manipulative?

5. Recall one of your most joyful moments. Describe both your internal experience and your external expression in that moment.

6. Have there been times when you sensed dangers that the men around you dismissed or refused to hear? How did you respond?

7. Have you ever been part of a project you cared deeply about that was nearly derailed by someone else? If so, how did you respond?

8. What are some of your sacred places? Why are they sacred to you?

9. Do you hear a new invitation from God? Have you been reminded of an old calling? How will you act this week to echo the growing faith and confidence of our mentor Sarah?

CHAPTER EIGHT

Embracing Our Vulnerability, Growing in Strength

THE SYROPHOENICIAN WOMAN IN MARK 7:24-30

As women, we often mistake our vulnerability for a lack of strength. In the face of power struggles, we sometimes crumble. At first glance, Jesus' encounter with the Syrophoenician woman appears to be His only rebuke of a woman. Yet looking more closely, we see this Gentile woman growing stronger in faith as Jesus invites her to face, embrace, and transcend her vulnerability. What seems to be an insult becomes a tool in Jesus' wise hand, strengthening her through His challenging resistance.

To Consider . . .

What would you consider your greatest strength as a woman? What do you see as your greatest weakness or vulnerability? How do you feel about those strengths and vulnerabilities?

"I CAN'T believe they said no. I just can't believe it."

As Jane and I sat together in the small, well-lit room where we met each month for spiritual direction, it was easy to see she was really struggling. Her facial expression alternated between the tension of deeply felt anger and the flaccid, drawn look of someone experiencing profound grief.

"The church board voted last night. They decided not to allow us to start a support group for sexual-abuse survivors. I'm in shock." Jane's story flowed from her like an actively seeping wound. She spoke with passion about the specific needs of certain women in her church, grieving for each one as she spoke. She recounted how they had organized, had investigated a group in another city as a model, and were in the process of exploring resources for training when the decision came. Her words became crisp with anger as she explained that the all-male board felt that the need for such a group was less critical than the potential liability.

The door was shut, slammed shut. Jane felt no room for appeal. Her sense of personal rejection was acute, as if her particular passion were unacceptable to God. She took the board's denial of her request into her very soul, experiencing it as a denial of her personhood and unique vision for good. She questioned her vision, her burden for these women.

Something within Jane resonated with the "less than" message of the board's decision in a soul-diminishing way. Without the support of the authority structure around her, she could not imagine any other path on which to pursue her dream. She felt stuck, unable to move forward and unable to let go. Self-doubt gnawed at her soul. She hated the fact that as a woman, she felt she did not have the power to make it happen. She hated her vulnerability. She detested the power struggle.

Over the next few years as we met together, Jane often referred back to that painful experience. Sometimes she was filled with regret that she had not ventured outside the church to do more for those women. She felt shame for abandoning her vision. She wondered about her internalization of the board's decision. At times she was angry at the apparent lack of compassion and injustice, at the very idea of church authority. She raged against her vulnerability as one who chose to follow another's leadership. She mused about what might have happened if she had chosen to engage the power struggle, fighting fire with fire, rallying the women in protest. She thought about leaving the church but found herself too rooted there. Her children loved it there. The community loved her, and she loved them.

Willing to negotiate her own ambivalence well, she also openly admitted how much she had grown under the nurture and teaching of the very leadership board she now found herself grieving. As a woman who held a management position in a major corporation, she knew the need for structure and authority. She also knew well that authority was a part of how God had structured the church. We held the pain and unanswered questions together, hoping for a new way to see it all, waiting for a vision of healing.

Surprisingly, that vision began in the form of another no. Deborah, a close friend and fellow church member of Jane's, had recently been diagnosed with cancer. Jane's personal response to her friend's pain and fear birthed an idea for a healing service. Jane wanted to gather their church family for the specific purposes of demonstrating to Deborah how much she was loved and offering special prayers for her healing. After mentioning her thought to her pastor in passing the next day, he told her he didn't think it was a good idea but didn't have time to discuss it at that moment. Jane made an appointment for the next morning.

Jane recounted her experience: "When I sensed his resistance, everything in me began to shut down. I was thankful we couldn't talk more that day. Before we met, I had a chance to think everything through again, a piece at a time, and ground myself in a few things."

She continued, "For instance, I knew that the vision for the service was good. God invites us to ask for healing. Asking to do it at church was good, too. Deborah really needed all the support of the community.

Surprisingly, I even decided that authority, wanting to work through the pastor, was good. The boundaries and structure really are necessary and good—well, most of the time. Even before we met, I sensed a real strength in my gut. No matter what happened in the meeting, there were some things I was certain of.

"From the start of our meeting, I could tell he'd used the time since our first conversation in a much different way. He had marshaled his arguments and came out firing. He would not do for one what he could not do for all. No exceptions. Policy. Policy. Policy. All before I'd said a word! And, you know what, I just listened. Something inside me reminded me that he had the right to make the decision about whether we would do the service at the church or not. He'd been given that authority. He was trying as best he could to use the power he'd been given for good. I didn't hate him for that. And he had a point, though, in my opinion, not a very good one. I guess even more amazingly, I didn't hate myself for choosing to be at the whim of his decision-making process.

"In fact, for the first time, I felt that I wasn't at his whim at all. I was just sad that we couldn't really talk about this. There didn't seem to be any interest in real conversation." Jane paused. The silence seemed to validate the genuineness of her sorrow.

"But I had a sense that the vision was still good. The request was still valid. I certainly didn't apologize. The service would happen with him or without, at the church or somewhere else. In fact, I already had a plan B. I figured my garden space was sacred, too, and big enough to hold the whole church.

"For the first time, it was as though I saw a whole other world of power I could tap into. A different kind of system. One that had little to do with politics and policies and systems and authority and everything to do with love and mercy and goodness. I didn't need to back down; I didn't need to fight fire with fire. For the first time, I could imagine another way, a way that somehow went around or through or over that old system. It's almost as if the very things that make me vulnerable in one system make me powerful in the other. I don't know. I just know it worked."

Jane smiled and almost let out a giggle. "I think *I* shocked *him* this time. When he was done, all I did was affirm his right to make the call and said very simply that I saw things differently. I even thought to say, 'Policies are made for man, not man for policies.' Then I thanked him and left. I personally invited him to the service at my house. And he came! It was great!"

As we continued to talk, Jane spoke about the special prayer time and how healing it had been for her friend. She had written the service herself, using her intimate knowledge of Deborah to bless her in unique ways with thoughtful expressions of love. She spoke of poetry and candles and prayer, of oil and tears and healing laughter. She was especially grateful that she had found a way to negotiate genuine respect for authority and for herself, and she thanked God for the noble, healing vision He had given her.

The confident strength Jane now experienced in response to this second challenge was just as evident on her face as the distress had been years before. This second no had met with a very different woman, a woman of new faith and new strength, a woman who no longer hated or feared her vulnerability but instead saw it as an integral part of a new world of influence. Jane's presence radiated both the powerfully loving Spirit of God and a new, stronger sense of her own feminine soul. She even concluded our time that day celebrating the newfound respect she now felt from her pastor.

Through navigating both of these painful denials, Jane had discovered a new strength within. Her long-sought vision for healing had finally come. Together we celebrated her growing strength and the oddly shaped door of challenge through which it had arrived. Though we were surprised by that form of resistance training, it seems to be a tool God has used before for feminine growth.

AN ANCIENT WOMAN'S SOUL

The story of the Syrophoenician woman in Mark 7:24-30 comes at a breaking point in the book of Mark as Jesus left Galilee, venturing forth into less familiar Gentile territory. The reason for his shift in focus might have been the fact that the political climate of Israel had grown menacing, or maybe He was simply tired of the Jews' blindness. From what I have read, most scholars believe that this was not a missionary venture by intention but an effort to let things cool down after a direct confrontation with the Pharisees. Whatever the case, this encounter shows that Jesus never failed to notice real faith no matter where He found it.

A Hidden God

Jesus left that place and went to the vicinity of Tyre. He entered a house and did not want anyone to know it; yet he could not keep his presence secret. (verse 24)

From the very beginning of this story of Jesus' encounter with the Syrophoenician woman, our expectations of Jesus are challenged. Though Mark refers to Jesus' attempts at secrecy often, it is not a comfortable thought for most of us. It feels as if Jesus was hiding from people who needed Him. Clearly He was not successful in this passage, but the very idea that He would even try such a thing is most disturbing.

Though I have read many theological explanations, none of them satisfy my soul. From time to time, I still experience the hiddenness of Jesus: when heartfelt questions go unanswered, when needed miracles fail to materialize, when long-held dreams go unfulfilled, when effective ministries close their doors and hungry children remain unfed, when failing relationships continue to rip and tear at hearts. Though I know on some level it is never true, at times it feels as if Jesus is avoiding me.

Strength Does Not Equal Self-Reliance

In fact, as soon as she heard about him, a woman whose little daughter was possessed by an evil spirit came and fell at his feet. The woman was a Greek, born in Syrian Phoenicia. (verses 25-26)

From the moment she enters the story, we get a sense of this woman's strength. Though Jesus was not well-known in the region, having spent little time there, word of His healing powers made it at least as far as her door. Good news travels fast. The presence of a healer in her midst was definitely good news. Odds are good that this was all she knew of Jesus— that He was a new Rabbi with a reputation for healing. Her response was swift and decisive. She readily acknowledged her need for help, not always an easy admission. For this wise woman, strength did not mean doing it all herself but gathering the resources available to her.

But look at the situation again. Was it logical to think that Jesus would really be available to her? Remember the customary Jewish bent toward exclusion? Who was she to expect that this Jewish Rabbi would have anything to do with her as a Gentile? She went to Jesus fully aware of the cultural, religious, and gender differences that would unavoidably be a part of any encounter. Such inequality left her wide open, vulnerable to abuse. She knew there was a very real likelihood of rejection. Nevertheless she went. She was a woman of uncommon strength.

Asking with Passion

She begged Jesus to drive the demon out of her daughter. (verse 26)

Picture the scene: a begging woman, fallen at the feet of Jesus. Not exactly the image most modern women would paint as a shining example of strength. For most of us, the idea of begging is inextricably connected to an internal perception filled with self-demeaning, self-diminishing, self-depreciating, self-degrading thoughts and void of any sense of personal dignity. And that is often the case. Remember how the woman with the hemorrhage approached Jesus from behind and below in a hidden fashion? Later we saw that such a posture did indeed reflect an inner sense of invisibility that needed more healing.

This however, is a very different kind of story. There is little evidence of such a mindset in this woman from Syrian Phoenicia. As we read on, we will see that she could hold her own even in a pretty challenging conversation. Could there be another explanation for such an approach?

Perhaps this woman's choice to come begging was motivated more by her wisdom and intense passion for her cause than by her lack of dignity. Few things, if any, strike more centrally to a woman's heart than the well-being of her children. As is sometimes said, "Some things are worth begging for." Her single-mindedness and focused passion were parts of her strength.

Interestingly, it may have been her great internal confidence in her own dignity that allowed her to take such an extreme approach. Rather than fighting the existing system of inequality, she chose to use it. She accepted her place of vulnerability, grounded herself in her dignity, and moved forward with faith. Uncompromising in her goal, she compromised in her approach, not as a victim but as a wise woman with a plan. She knew that her dignity was internal and could not be lost in a moment of begging for her daughter's healing.

Her bold approach also evidenced her great faith. If she did not believe Jesus could help her daughter, why endure such humiliation? Why even waste her time? Even on her knees, this was a woman of great internal strength and enormous faith.

Resistance Training

"First let the children eat all they want," he told her, "for it is not right to take the children's bread and toss it to their dogs." (verse 27)

Say what? Did Jesus just call this poor, desperate, Gentile mother a dog? Well, yes. Considering how this response flies in the face of Jesus' other compassion-filled interactions with women (and other marginalized or hurting folk), it warrants a deeper look.

Let's first look at the theological context. The fact that Jesus walked and ministered primarily among the Jews is historical fact. It is as if God chose to give them the first and best shot to believe. We tend to bristle against such apparent inequality in the work of God. It is one of those uncomfortable realities most of us avoid. Yet it is definitely a reality throughout Scripture. The fact that God chose the few for the good of all often brings us little comfort. Clearly God's choice was not based on merit. God chose whom God chose. God favors whom God favors. There are "children," and there are "dogs." Ugh.

Let's look a bit deeper. What exactly bothers us so? Perhaps something within us rages against such inequality or, more precisely, fears it because we know that inequality is a setup for injustice. Systemic power differences make those who find themselves labeled as less powerful more susceptible to abuse. As women who are often greatly aware of our significant vulnerability, this is a key gender-specific challenge to growth for us.

Most women readily acknowledge greater physical and emotional vulnerability when compared to men. We like to hit our golf balls from the tees closer to the holes; it is only fair. We smile when men laugh at us for crying at Hallmark commercials. But we are often less willing to admit or address our greater social and religious vulnerability. Many times "good ole boys" outside the church are still "good ole boys" within the church. There are existing power structures in place that refuse, fail, or struggle to regard us as women. We are sometimes unseen, sometimes excluded. We are vulnerable.

And when in the course of life our greater vulnerability becomes connected to neglect, abuse, and pain, many of us begin to struggle with, run from, hate, or even completely deny that aspect of our feminine souls. We see our vulnerability as a liability. We harden tender parts of our hearts, assuming this is our only defense against more pain.

Though we seldom realize it, much is lost in that moment of self-protection. Far from a liability, our feminine vulnerability is a real relational asset. It makes us easier to trust, easier to approach, and easier to connect with. As those with less authority, we are often deemed less powerful and therefore less threatening. This can be a huge advantage relationally. Our experiences on the receiving end of injustice, inequality, and prejudice also have the potential to make us much more compassionate. Choosing to live in the reality of our vulnerability is both a challenge and a matter of feminine integrity. If we surrender our vulnerability, much is lost.

Learning to deal well with the vulnerability of our feminine souls is a critically important growth issue for most women. As I have said before, I believe Jesus had keen, gender-specific knowledge of spirituality. In this story, Jesus led this woman down an unusual path to growth of strength through acceptance of vulnerability. In His challenge to her, He not only highlighted her greater vulnerability as a Gentile; you might say He almost rubbed her nose in it. Yet it is clear that His intent was never to make her less powerful but rather to offer her yet another glimpse of this path to enduring power that He Himself had chosen.

It is an intriguing thought that Jesus chose the vulnerability we as women so often run from. Consider His birth. He was a human infant, born in a stable, poor, homeless, illegitimate, and sought by a king for destruction. How vulnerable can you get? Consider His earthly ministry. He did not engage or support the religious powers that be but instead continually criticized them. His constant focus was on changing hearts, the internal beliefs and "power structures." Consider His death. The One who could have called down ten thousand angels in His defense healed the ear of the soldier who came to arrest Him. Over and over, He chose to live vulnerably, counting on God to make His way. Over and over, the power of God was demonstrated through His choice to embrace His vulnerability.

In this moment with a Gentile woman of faith, He sought to help her better understand the source of true and lasting power. On some level, she already understood that not all power comes through the door of authority structures. She would never have come to Jesus if she had not already believed that mercy and love could be stronger than any social or religious power structure. Though she may not have had any language for it, she was very connected to this alternative power grid. In fact, she was banking on it big-time.

Through challenging her, Jesus sought to strengthen her and give voice to what she knew intuitively. One of the latest fads in physical fitness for women is known as resistance training. The use of weights or other forms of resistance allows muscle to be built and toned more effectively. The same dynamic seems to be true for our souls. Or as Matthew Henry puts it, "Where Christ knows the faith of poor supplicants to be strong, he sometimes delights to try it and put it to the stretch."[1] As we have repeatedly seen before in His interactions with women, Jesus gave this woman a chance to express to the world around her an amazingly strong faith. In doing so, He instilled in her forever the soul-freeing truth that being "less than" before men in no way translates to being "less than" before God. As Jesus drew her out, even through what appeared at first to be an insult, we once again see feminine growth manifested as a woman coming to a fuller and stronger sense of voice.

Saying Yes to Vulnerability, No to Powerlessness

"Yes, Lord," she replied, "but even the dogs under the table eat the children's crumbs." (verse 28)

I would have loved to have been a fly on the wall in this moment, to have heard the words spoken, seen the facial expressions exchanged, felt the tone of the room. My imagination tells me this strong woman looked up straight into the eyes of Jesus as she replied. In fact, I think they were both smiling, that kind of wry, knowing smile that said they both knew a secret that most people around them failed to grasp.

If we listen only to her words, we are startled to hear her acceptance of both inequality and personal insult. Jesus clearly placed her on the "less favored" side of that unequal equation. Such acceptance offends us.

But even as she accepted the inequality and its inherent vulnerability, she denied its power over her request. That denial of power is key. She stood her ground, unwavering in her focus and her request. By faith, she believed that healing, love, mercy, compassion, and goodness were more powerful forces than lack of standing in any social or religious system, even a system set up by this healing Rabbi's God.

This woman held a uniquely feminine power that operated outside the realm of an authority structure and politics. It is a kind of power that embraces and even uses our greater vulnerability and plays to our strengths as women because it is rooted in our ability to form strong relational connections. Though such connections are not exclusively feminine, they do tend to be made more readily by women. This Syrophoenician woman possessed a strength that was rooted not in formal structures or systems but in her long-standing relationship with her daughter and her new relationship with Jesus. Knowing and owning her feminine power allowed her to stand tall in the midst of seeming rejection, grounded in the goodness of her calling from God and her confidence in Jesus.

She cared not how this system labeled her, favored child or dog. Again, we do not get a sense that she did not care because she was self-depreciating but because she was strong. She knew her strength and dignity were so internal, grounded in her very soul, that no external force or label could change them.

She was operating from a totally different power grid, a paradigm unstopped by personal insult, inequality, or even injustice. It is the power grid of the gospel that Jesus lived before us and sought to help us understand. He did not use politics or structural authority to change the world; He used relationships and chose vulnerability, love, mercy, and goodness. Authority structures are God-ordained and necessary. They are also vulnerable to corruption. Yet even power in the hands of evil is ultimately powerless against good. It can reshape the physical form of life and work, but even then God can use it for good. Rather than an excuse to stop, this challenge became a form of resistance that only made this Gentile woman stronger.

Like Jesus, she did not need to play external games with social systems. She, too, remained focused on her mission. Though some were called to battle injustices, that was not her cause at this time. She accepted and then transcended her experience of insult, vulnerability, and inequality, confident in the mercy and healing power of God.

Grounded in a Vision

Then he told her, "For such a reply, you may go; the demon has left your daughter." (verse 29)

Jesus heard her reply in all of its wisdom, faith, and power. She had grounded herself in a vision for healing and help and an expectation of mercy when she set out from home. She and Jesus both understood with deep clarity where real power lies. Even in the face of existing social and religious systems, she would not let go of that belief in goodness.

Jesus' response was brief, granting this strong and needy woman's one request. If we read this story superficially, the literal language seems to be moving in one direction and the action in the other. Her begging posture, Jesus' insult, and her acceptance of it seem to say there's no help here. Yet this verse forces us to go back and reinterpret this interaction at a deeper level, one that is intuitive more than stated. Again, we sense the backward, upside-down, in-a-mirror wordless world of feminine spirituality.

Note especially that Jesus connected the daughter's healing directly to this mother's wise and strong reply. He seemed to know that if He had not offered the healing she requested, she would not have left. Again, He specifically and intentionally affirmed her voice, personhood, and impact. As He did consistently with the women He encountered, He did not let her leave without a stronger sense of her feminine soul.

Foundations of Strength

She went home and found her child lying on the bed, and the demon gone. (verse 30)

The Syrophoenician woman is like so many women of faith in Scripture. She is strong and bold; willing to love and risk; at peace with her vulnerability; sure of her power, wisdom, and vision; asking passionately for what she needs; living fully the glory of her feminine soul.

Though she entered this story in strength, she left even stronger. How would she have known, really known, that love and mercy are stronger than inequality and authority structures except for a moment like this? Her faith and ours are built on the foundation of stories of God's miraculous work in our lives. As she dared to believe in Jesus, to believe that even personal and social vulnerability could not stop her vision for good, her faith was tangibly and clearly affirmed. Jesus' resistance-training program was effective in her life.

My guess is that Jesus was refreshed by this encounter. He spent many soul-wearying days seeking to give His power-hungry disciples just a glimpse of the mercy-and love-centered power dynamic. Even to the end, they never seemed to "get it." Perhaps because women have been on the powerless end of social and religious structures for so long, we tend to be able to see these less obvious, nonauthoritarian power dynamics more easily and utilize them more effectively. Maybe that is a hidden gift of our greater vulnerability, redeeming a bit of the pain we suffer.

Anytime we encounter injustice, inequality, and abusive power, it is critical to remember that mercy and love are still stronger. Jesus is still our way to "leap over" the one to get to the other. He still invites us to ground ourselves in what we know and dare to believe in that which we cannot always see. It is the gospel message of old lived out in our feminine souls today. He asks each of us to bring our particular vision for good to Him, willing to be trained, even with resistance, and trusting His way to help us discover our strength as women. Even now, I can hear Jesus celebrating the Syrophoenician woman's wisdom and strength as she walked out the door. Even now, I can hear Him applauding Jane's newfound resilience. Can you?

YOUR JOURNEY

For personal reflection and group discussion

1. Describe your current image of a strong woman.

2. Describe a circumstance when you had a vision for doing good and met a wall of criticism, injustice, or opposition. How did you

respond, both internally (thoughts and feelings) and externally (actions and choices)?

3. Have you ever felt as if Jesus were avoiding you? Describe the experience.

4. Recall your description of a strong woman. Does your image include neediness, vulnerability, love, and mercy, or is it more grounded in traditional views of strength, such as power and independence?

5. Have you ever begged for something? Describe the experience. What in your life right now would be worthy of begging?

6. When have you felt challenged by God, as if you were in a resistance-training program of sorts? Describe both the experience and your response.

7. What inequalities or injustices do you struggle with most often? In what situations do you feel powerless? How do you generally respond?

8. Have there been moments in your life when you were able to "leap over" or transcend injustice for the sake of a greater cause? Describe the experiences and their impact on your life.

9. What helps you find your ground in the face of criticism or injustice?

10. Is there currently a situation in your life that is calling for a new understanding of power or a deeper awareness of strength?

CHAPTER NINE

Exploring Our Seasons,
Growing Through Our Experience and Intuition

NAOMI IN RUTH 1–2

In the midst of an Old Testament filled with men led by the specific revelation of God, we find Naomi, a woman whose relationship with God was grounded deeply in His broader, more general revelation of life experience. This more feminine experience of God, guided by intuition and a different way of seeing the circumstances and situations of life, is considered by some as dangerous, bordering on heresy. Though the more specific Word of God adds essential completion of truth for women, the feminine soul grows as we, like Naomi, live with an acute awareness of God in our experiences—the seasons and rhythms within and without.

To Consider . . .

Have you ever had an experience of the Divine "speaking" to you through creation or through the way life has unfolded around you? If so, describe that encounter.

LIKE the seasons that shift around us quite apart from our control, internal seasons of change often enter our lives uninvited. Several years ago, my husband and I and our three children, ages eleven, eight, and five, moved back to Texas from St. Croix in the Virgin Islands. We had been there two years for my husband's job. We had a marvelous time on the island, but after two years of my husband's coping with a very stressful job assignment, we knew it was time to come home. Relocating to the same city, same house, same church, same friends we had left just twenty-four months before, I discovered to my great surprise that I was not the same woman. Though there had been adjustments in both directions, the ones on the move there felt "downhill," easy. The ones coming back to Texas felt *huge*. I think my soul is better suited to island living!

After enjoying a much simpler life in the Caribbean for many months, I found it impossible to resume my previous hectic schedule. For two years, I spent more time on the beach than at the mall. If Woolworth's didn't have it, it was not to be found. Because it did not take long to explore an island twenty-seven miles by seven miles, I invested much more in relationships than in events or experiences. Every afternoon a neighbor and I enjoyed coffee together as our children played outside. I went to church in a plantation great house with three-foot-thick walls and tamarind trees just outside the unpaned windows. I learned to garden in a climate where my hibiscus (or "biscuit flowers," as my three-year-old called them) bloomed all year. And I hit golf balls on an elevated driving range into a rainforest valley. It was an awesome spot!

Somewhere along the way, my perceptions and priorities had shifted without my realizing anything at all was changing. For the first time, billboards offended me, seen as visual intrusions shouting uninvited messages. I missed my time with my neighbor. I wanted to garden rather than leave home for another Bible study meeting. I wanted to get my hands dirty—to plant, nurture, and enjoy my own small patch of earth.

It was very difficult for me to choose to listen to these changes within, to honor these new desires. Friends were noticing the differences and asking questions. I couldn't explain what I did not yet understand myself. Reluctantly following this new path at first, I soon was poring over books and magazines, visiting nurseries and gardens, beginning to shape a plan for my long-neglected yard.

As I put dreams on paper, one of my highest priorities was that my garden would be visually appealing year-round. I envisioned only evergreen plants. Yet the realities of my limited budget found me planting a great deal of lantana, a native Texas shrub that my mother and mother-in-law offered me in abundance and free of charge. Though very tolerant of our beastly hot summers, the lantana was anything but evergreen, dying back to mangled, brittle, brown twigs after the first freeze. It was just as ugly as I imagined it would be.

To make matters worse, our first winter back was an unusually harsh one. For the first time on record, the southeast corner of Texas experienced a devastating ice storm. More accustomed to tropical weather events, my husband aptly described this natural disaster as a "hurricane in slow motion." With the power off and little hope of rapid restoration, our small family huddled close to one another and our fireplace.

I felt an odd connection with winter that year. This was the winter I referenced briefly in chapter 5, the season in which I first began reading, reflecting, and simply being still enough for some sense of self-awareness to be born within. I have often been amused that God had to take me two thousand miles from home and drop me in a Caribbean culture just to slow me down enough to hear His voice (may you be so blessed!). Having begun to explore some of my surprising internal changes, I was beginning to see that I had spent an entire lifetime avoiding grief, running from anything remotely akin to a "winter of the soul." An entire dimension of my own story had been hidden from me, disallowed into my conscious experience. Whether it was pain from neighborhood girlfriend spats or rejection from old boyfriends or disappointments in my marriage or grief from foolish decisions, all sadness had been refused. All tears remained uncried. My garden plan permitting only evergreen plants was a reflection of how I had lived my life thus far.

To make matters worse, I was just beginning to recognize the profound depth of my newfound grief for having lived so much of my life completely out of touch with my own feminine soul. I was thirty-five and just discovering the wonders of being a woman! I had missed so very much that could not be regained or replaced. As the severe winter continued around me, the climate within felt at least as harsh.

The second afternoon of our ice storm, I ventured out into my garden, preferring the risk of falling limbs to the noise of my cabin fever–afflicted threesome of children. With the grass crunching beneath my shoes, I surveyed the damage. Unexpectedly, the sun broke through the hovering clouds for the first time. The seemingly dead lantana before me was instantly transformed into brilliant shafts of crystal, artfully displayed as if arranged by a gifted sculptor. I literally stopped in my icy tracks, awed by the beauty of winter.

In that moment of worship, something deep inside my soul shifted. For the first time, I saw the season of winter in my garden more completely. Yes, there is pain and loss, brown branches and brittle stems. But there is also beauty and wonder, glorious crystal shafts dancing in the sunlight.

Immediately, the unfolding season around me began to educate my own life story. I knew that in my winter of the soul, I could also find beauty if I would just look for it. In seeing with new eyes the season that enfolded me, I could begin to see the season of my feminine soul with a greater wisdom than ever before. God as Creator nurtured me that day, sharing wisdom with me in a healing moment. More confident that I could find beauty in my grief, I felt a new willingness to abide with the pain as long as it needed to last. I would refuse to rush spring.

This experience of listening more broadly to the voice of God in the world around me was new for me. I hesitated to share my story with others, feeling a bit embarrassed. I had been afraid to listen to anything but Scripture, lumping all experiential or intuitive spirituality into the category of raw emotion or that of New Age, neither of which I trusted as a reliable source of wisdom. When I did share my story, I often felt as if I needed to apologize for this new and different experience of God.

Though Scripture clearly teaches that God is revealed in creation (see Romans 1:20), I had never taken that truth seriously. Undeniably, God was opening new doors in my heart through these experiences, doors that Scripture alone had not accessed. I began to question my narrow approach to hearing the wisdom of God.

It just so happened that during that season, I was studying the book of Ruth. As I brought my garden experience to that book, I discovered that the women of that story honored their unique bent toward *experiencing* God in life, learning well the art of listening broadly to His voice in intuitive ways. I developed a special connection with Naomi. She, too, had known a harsh winter of the soul. As she became my mentor, I listened to her story closely. My life experience and uniquely feminine intuition, as well as observations about nature and myself, became a lens through which I saw even more in Naomi's story, found in Ruth 1–2.

AN ANCIENT WOMAN'S SOUL

Naomi lived "when the judges ruled." Though there were often courageous leaders at the helm, there were also wild stories told from that era, a time when "every man did what was right in his own eyes" (Judges 17:6, NASB). For Naomi and her family, that meant moving to the foreign nation of Moab during a famine in their country of Judah.

The Chill of Winter Arrives

In the days when the judges ruled, there was a famine in the land, and a man from Bethlehem in Judah, together with his wife and two sons, went to live for a while in the country of Moab. The man's name was Elimelech, his wife's name Naomi, and the names of his two sons were Mahlon and Kilion. They were Ephrathites from Bethlehem, Judah. And they went to Moab and lived there.

Now Elimelech, Naomi's husband, died, and she was left with her two sons. They married Moabite women, one named Orpah and the other Ruth. After they had lived there about ten

years, both Mahlon and Kilion also died, and Naomi was left
without her two sons and her husband. (1:1-5)

As a chaplain, I have encountered many individuals like Naomi who have
experienced tragedy upon tragedy, loss upon loss, grief upon grief. These
are people whose lives are suddenly emptied of all that once held
meaning. The depth of their pain could never fully be expressed in words.

Imagine Naomi's devastation: widowed in a foreign country and
experiencing the death of both her children. The last blow was an
especially painful one. The death of a child is always an agonizing grief,
wrenching the heart in strange ways with a stark sense that the whole
world is out of order. Multiple losses emptied this woman's life.

I have experienced multiplied loss only in brief moments and only
with much smaller losses. Though my grief has been minor by
comparison, the reality is that none of us experience our losses on a
comparative basis. Most of us will not, thankfully, experience the kind of
devastation Naomi faced. Yet we will face losses, significant losses,
losses that invite us into a winter of mourning. It is tempting to dismiss
our lesser griefs, to hide behind the more devastating experiences of
others. Tempting, yet unwise. Winter, harsh or mild, is a reality in all
years and in all stories.

Shifting Seasons Without and Within

When she heard in Moab that the Lord had come to the aid of
his people by providing food for them, Naomi and her daughters-
in-law prepared to return home from there. With her two
daughters-in-law she left the place where she had been living and
set out on the road that would take them back to the land of
Judah.

Then Naomi said to her two daughters-in-law, "Go back,
each of you, to your mother's home. May the Lord show kindness
to you, as you have shown to your dead and to me. May the Lord
grant that each of you will find rest in the home of another
husband."

Then she kissed them and they wept aloud and said to her,
"We will go back with you to your people."

But Naomi said, "Return home, my daughters. Why would
you come with me? Am I going to have any more sons, who could
become your husbands? Return home, my daughters; I am too old
to have another husband. Even if I thought there was still hope
for me—even if I had a husband tonight and then gave birth to
sons—would you wait until they grew up? Would you remain
unmarried for them? No, my daughters. It is more bitter for me
than for you, because the Lord's hand has gone out against me!"

At this they wept again. Then Orpah kissed her mother-in-
law good-by, but Ruth clung to her. (verses 6-14)

Naomi heard that in Bethlehem the season was shifting. Where there once
was famine, there now was food. For Naomi, that provision was directly
connected to the presence of God. In those days, God sometimes
disciplined Judah by sending famine to their land. The blessing of God
was closely tied to the productivity of the land. This shift in the world
around her was part of what prompted the shift within Naomi's soul. As
she listened to the seasons changing, perhaps she longed to be part of a
new rhythm. Bethlehem was still home for Naomi. Even though she had
lived in Moab for a decade, she never lost her sense of home. Like many
of us, when we are hurting, we run for home. Naomi did the same.

Naomi's way of being led by God stands in sharp contrast to the norm
of the Old Testament. Moses talked to God on a mountain. Samuel heard
God's voice in the night. David heard God speak through prophets. The
prophets often received word-for-word messages to pass on to the nation.
The communication was direct, clear, exact, and word-centered—very
different from Naomi's guiding internal inclinations.

Naomi's leading was intuitively sensed. She listened broadly to life
around her. Some may struggle to see such conclusions as adequately
supported by this text. I suggest, however, that this book, in which
intuitive women are the actors and God's hidden hand is the motivating
force, is actually meant to be read and interpreted intuitively. Though we
should never be careless in our scholarship or move outside the

boundaries of what the Text can say, I think that given the tone of this book, these conclusions are within bounds.

Like the kings and prophets, Naomi was following God. This move home was about more than familiar sights and smells or a culture that affirmed her identity; it was the residence of her God. Unlike Christians today who see God as always present, the Jews saw God as much more connected to a place: the Promised Land, the temple, the cloud, and so on. An individual's relationship with God was predominantly, though not exclusively, tied to the community experience of worship and sacrificial rites. For Naomi, to return home meant to reengage a more active relationship with her God.

Notice how she referred to her current perspective on that relationship: "The LORD's hand has gone out against me!" She did not exactly count God among her friends at this juncture. Yet this was the same God whose blessing she was seeking for her beloved daughters-in-law. Ambivalent at best, back to the land of the Lord Naomi went. Naomi listened to her feminine intuition. Wisely, she listened more to the shifting seasons and yearning draw of home within her soul than the painful struggle to make sense of her suffering that raged in her mind.

It is important to note a Jewish custom to better understand the specifics of Naomi's loss of hope reflected in verses 11-13. It was customary for the brother or nearest relative of a deceased man to take the new widow into his home for the sake of bearing children in his dead relative's name. This custom, known as levirate marriage, allowed the lineage of the deceased to continue beyond the grave.

That continuance was important to Naomi personally because it was her assurance, through the lives of her children and their offspring, of a part in God's work in the world. It was not only her husband and children who had died, but also her hope of a meaningful place in the history of her people. So it was with great grief that Naomi negated the possibility of grandchildren as she exhorted her companions to return to their native homes. Too old to bear more sons, Naomi saw no chance of future generations assuaging her loss.

Seeing Beauty in Winter

*"Look," said Naomi, "your sister-in-law is going back to her
people and her gods. Go back with her."*

*But Ruth replied, "Don't urge me to leave you or to turn
back from you. Where you go I will go, and where you stay I will
stay. Your people will be my people and your God my God.
Where you die I will die, and there I will be buried. May the
Lord deal with me, be it ever so severely, if anything but death
separates you and me." When Naomi realized that Ruth was
determined to go with her, she stopped urging her. (verses 15-18)*

This passage has intrigued me for years. I have always wondered why it
is so often used at weddings (including my own) when the context is a
relationship between two women. Though clearly Ruth was a prime
example of loyalty, I also believe she was a woman who had eyes to see
the beauty of winter.

Think about what she saw in Naomi. In the midst of her own
unspeakable pain, Naomi sought good for Ruth, who was suffering from
her own loss. The blessing from the previous section revealed Naomi's
enduring love for her daughter-in-law.

Ruth also must have seen Naomi's courage. Attempting an
international move as a widow was no small feat. Deeper still, Naomi
possessed the rare courage to honestly live before others in the midst of
her grief, to refuse to hide any part of her life. She spoke about life as she
experienced it, present to the love and the pain, the intimate attachments
and the feelings of abandonment.

In the midst of bitterness, Ruth could see sweetness. Again, her
feminine intuition and insight beyond the easily observable is the most
likely explanation. Ruth knew the whole of Naomi, not just the Naomi of
this moment. She could see that in the midst of devastation, Naomi was
not only still standing; she was on the move. Though Naomi was blind to
the beauty of her winter, Ruth was not.

Notice Ruth's confession. She focused on remaining with Naomi.
Though her words reveal a personal relationship with and belief in God,

her vow was not focused on God but instead on this bitter, grieving woman. Having found a source of love and wisdom in Naomi, a woman noble and authentic enough to meet even the harsh season of winter head-on, Ruth was not about to let her go.

Embracing Winter

So the two women went on until they came to Bethlehem. When they arrived in Bethlehem, the whole town was stirred because of them, and the women exclaimed, "Can this be Naomi?"

"Don't call me Naomi" [meaning "pleasant"], she told them. "Call me Mara [meaning "bitter"], because the Almighty has made my life very bitter. I went away full, but the Lord has brought me back empty. Why call me Naomi? The Lord has afflicted me; the Almighty has brought misfortune upon me." (verses 19-21)

Did Naomi really speak of God like that? Yes. And even more telling, God made sure the community recorded her words so we would know it. Often I talk with hurting people who are so afraid to be honest about their feelings, especially their feelings about God. God is not afraid of our raw emotions.

Naomi did two things: She renamed herself, and she renamed her perception of God. To the Jews, naming was a big deal. Technically, as a woman she did not have the authority to name or rename anyone. Yet in this moment of deep pain, we sense great determination and power in Naomi's words.

Interestingly, when we run from painful feelings of loss, we diminish our sense of personhood. When my grief was hidden from me, I was less of a woman. Though we often feel as if grief will diminish us (for instance, "melting into a puddle of tears" or "falling apart"), the opposite is true. It is the avoidance of grief that makes us less than we truly are. Naomi's unadulterated sorrow was growing her as a woman, enlarging her feminine soul as well as her understanding of God. Again, we get a sense of growth birthed through pain, a natural, albeit difficult, process unfolding before us. A uniquely feminine process.

Naomi lived into her winter with courageous honesty. She boldly acknowledged that these losses had changed both her identity and her understanding of God forever. Loss has a way of doing that. In wisdom, Naomi embraced her winter, changing her name and inviting her grief into every aspect of her life.

Seeds of Spring

So Naomi returned from Moab accompanied by Ruth the Moabitess, her daughter-in-law, arriving in Bethlehem as the barley harvest was beginning.

Now Naomi had a relative on her husband's side, from the clan of Elimelech, a man of standing, whose name was Boaz.

And Ruth the Moabitess said to Naomi, "Let me go to the fields and pick up the leftover grain behind anyone in whose eyes I find favor."

Naomi said to her, "Go ahead, my daughter." (1:22–2:2)

It is no mistake that the two books in the Bible named for women, Ruth and Esther, have a similar sense of God at work. In both books, God is more the undercurrent than the obvious force, working in hidden, covert ways, shifting seasons and using oh-so-ordinary means to accomplish extraordinary things. In fact, God is not directly spoken of at all in Esther. In Ruth, we see over and over God's "ordinary" miracles through things that "just so happened."

As is reflected in these two books, our feminine experience of God is often subtle, broad, and inclusive of all facets of life. We see God all around us and learn to look for Him in unusual places. We hear God's voice in a wide variety of ways, attributing power to the ordinary parts of our daily routine. Just as in other aspects of life, we are often intuitive in our spirituality.

For example, notice how the women "just happened" to arrive at the start of harvest. This was a new season for Judah, a season of abundance after many years of famine. Working through this physical season, God was also at work behind the scenes, planting the seeds of a new season of abundance for Naomi. Later, we discover that Ruth "just happened" to choose the field of Boaz, a close relative with the potential to act on the levirate marriage referenced previously. On one level, Ruth was just doing the next logical thing. Like planting seeds in spring, it seemed so small. But with God, "the next logical thing" can be the seed of something very big, the first sign of spring, an "ordinary" miracle in the making.

Note once more the contrast of this kind of vague yet valid spiritual leading with the clear directives presented in most of the Old Testament. This book of women and God is different. It is amazing how easily that difference can be seen once we tune our eyes to it. How healing to know that God knows and affirms our unique experience of Him.

Living as Mara, Naomi was blind to many things. In the midst of her experience of God's hand moving against her, His hidden hand moved on her behalf. Though she was aware enough to return to Bethlehem, there was much about this season she did not yet understand. But Naomi was listening, aware of the shifting season, open to God's voice even in a season of struggle. The author notes for us that Ruth went out only after receiving permission from her mother-in-law. Even in her confusion and pain, Naomi was an active participant in God's plan of blessing.

I invite you to walk through the remainder of the book of Ruth, looking for more evidence of the rhythm of spring—a season of grace, nourishment, and receiving. As the story continues to unfold, the seasons change. We can see themes of summer in the time of Naomi and Ruth's active collaborating with God's plan, characterized by bold and passionately "hot" moves. Summer was also that season of trusting another to grow what they could not, of consciously leaning on God and waiting for Him to act. And finally came autumn, a time of harvest and celebration, rich bounty beyond anything Naomi could have imagined. With each shift of season, we see Naomi's willingness to shift personally as she lived her experience authentically and in touch with her feminine soul.

One of the gifts for me as I entered that first harsh winter back in Texas was learning to use my bent toward a more experiential, intuitive spirituality as a tool for spiritual growth. Emboldened by Naomi, I quit apologizing and began exploring with wide-open eyes the messages God might want to give me through my surroundings and my instincts. I formed the habit of walking in my garden when I was anxious, applying quite literally Jesus' call to "consider the lilies" (Luke 12:27, NASB). I learned many deep spiritual truths as I observed how my plants grew—or, in some cases, did not grow. Our faithful God met me there time after time.

God began to weave Scripture and experience together in my life, one enhancing the other, offering greater fullness, wisdom, and balance to my life and spiritual growth. Life experience without the guiding wisdom of the Bible could easily be misread. That broader voice is more vague, more easily misunderstood. Likewise, my experiences enhanced my reading of Scripture, allowing me to see the Bible with more color and opening my intuitive understanding to many insights I would have missed. Even today, the ongoing dialogue of experience and Text keeps my spiritual life vital and challenging.

That long season of winter was followed several years later by a wild and unexpected spring. For me, that next season of grace, nourishment, and receiving was lived out in graduate school in the far-off land of the Northwest—well, far-off for a Texan. As I entered a new season of my life, I actively explored the themes of spring by planting bulbs and buying pictures of images of spring. I consciously used the season around me to inform the season within me.

As women, we have a wealth of unique life rhythms to explore: our monthly cycles, menopause, and, for most, pregnancy, labor, and delivery. Also, many of us have various seasons of relationship: singleness; marriage; motherhood with infants, toddlers, school-age children, and teens; the time of being a grandmother; and possibly even divorce or widowhood. Some of us have career stages as well. Sometimes we see these rhythms more as intrusions to our ordered spiritual lives than the gifts they can be, potentially burgeoning with wisdom.

I invite you to become more acutely aware of these rhythms, to speak about them, and to use them to inform your life and your reading of Scripture. These natural processes are an important part of God's revelation to us and are not to be neglected or unnoticed. Living with a greater awareness of them allows us to live more holistically and in tune with our experience, thus avoiding the ever-present temptation of hiding some parts of our souls.

YOUR JOURNEY

For personal reflection and group discussion

1. Name some of the natural rhythms currently at work in your life: internal rhythms (biological, emotional, spiritual, and so on) and external cadences surrounding you.

2. Describe your current life experience in terms of a season: summer, winter, spring, or fall. In what ways do your physical experiences and memories of the natural season help you find a vision for how to grow in this internal season of your life?

3. For most of us, winter is the most challenging season to negotiate. As best you can, name all the losses you have experienced in the last twelve months, large or small.

4. Describe your general response to grief and situations of loss. Do you embrace, dismiss, dramatize, negate via comparison, deny, medicate, explore?

5. Tell about a moment of beauty you have spotted in your own or another's winter. Describe individuals you have known who have lived winter well.

6. Reflect on a past "winter of the soul" in your life. How did spring dawn for you? Recall as many small details as you can.

7. Describe an "ordinary" miracle from your life, a time when God orchestrated events in such a way as to create a miracle using oh-so-ordinary tools.

8. How do you generally regard the changing rhythms of your life? What rhythms do you connect with most at this moment?

9. How will you choose to more actively use your experience and intuition as tools for spiritual growth?

Part Three

FEMININE SOULS IN SERVICE

CHAPTER TEN

Transforming Through Our Kindness, Offering Our Vision

RUTH IN RUTH 1–4

Ruth's simple acts of kindness transformed the lives of Naomi and Boaz, laying a foundation for God's work in generations to come. In contrast to the battle stories of the Old Testament in which men fought to advance God's purposes, we find Ruth's subtle, relational vision for kindness equally effective in moving God's cause forward. As women, we are often tempted to dismiss our more subtle styles of ministry as insignificant or less than the more direct approaches of men. If we listen well to Ruth, we will be inspired to once again embrace our unique vision for the power and place of kindness in God's work.

To Consider . . .

List as many acts of kindness as you can recall from the past week, both those you offered and those you received. Now, imagine your week without these moments. How would your experience of the week have been different?

DOING routine visits as a hospital chaplain sometimes feels like playing the lottery: During most visits, I make a small contribution, but every now and then, I hit the "jackpot." My visit with Mrs. Burton was one of those "jackpot" moments.

As I entered her hospital room, I found Mrs. Burton just getting settled. Her daughter had left to get her a few belongings because she had come to the doctor not expecting a hospital admission. She was anticipating a long afternoon alone, knowing that her daughter would not return for several hours. Feeling more bored than ill or uncomfortable due to the infected sore on her right arm, she was eager to talk.

I could tell right away that Mrs. Burton was a deep East Texas woman through and through. She was in her early seventies and spoke with a thick Southern accent, using simple words and a direct approach. Her hair was gray and tousled, her skin tanned and wrinkled. Her most beautiful feature was her smile, quick on her lips and free in expression.

It was not long until she had drawn me into one of the most beautiful stories I have ever heard. Though I do not recall how the subject came up, Mrs. Burton began by saying that her middle daughter, Susan, had died at age six after being diagnosed with a brain tumor only six months before her death. Mrs. Burton began to recount that life-changing journey not in terms of tragedies but in the language of kindnesses received.

First, there was the doctor. They knew little about this woman who was seeing their daughter for the first time after a sudden seizure. Mrs. Burton remembered that as she delivered these young parents the devastating news of their daughter's cancer, this kind woman had tears in her eyes. And as she talked about possible treatment options and prognosis, she listened to them as much as educated them. My new friend painted tender word pictures of this kind physician holding Susan on her knee.

Months later, Mrs. Burton continued, that same doctor informed them that the treatments were not working. After a multiweek stay in the hospital, Susan was allowed a brief trip home. She had begged repeatedly, and finally the doctor consented. Careful to warn Mrs. Burton and her husband that this respite from the hospital might well be very brief, she gave Susan a loving hug on her way out the door. "She was such a kind woman." Mrs. Burton said, sighing deeply. She then went on with her story.

"My mother-in-law was there when we got home, surrounded by our five other children. Susan jumped in her arms as she came through the door and then just as quickly ran off in the other room with her brothers and sisters. In minutes they were playing as if they'd never missed a beat."

As Mrs. Burton continued, she smiled warmly. "I could tell Gram was tired by the circles under her eyes. Taking over a household like ours was not an easy task for anyone, never mind a woman seventy-plus! Her eyes told one story, but her smile told me another. She could have gone home to rest, but she said she wasn't about to miss a minute of this night. Putting on a pot of coffee, she watched and listened all night to those kids playing. We both stayed up all night. I really appreciated her being there."

Silence lingered for a few minutes, as if the memories were too big for words. Only images in her mind could play them out. Eyes filling with soft tears, she began again. "That was some night. I think my kids lived a lifetime together in that one night. You know, they're all over forty now, but every year on Susan's birthday, they still talk about that night. They remember it like yesterday—the toys, the games, what they said, how they laughed. It's amazing.

"The sun wasn't up long when we heard a scream in the other room. I knew what had happened even before I went in. Another seizure, and off we went, back to the hospital. It was a while after we got back before they let us see her. They had her on a machine this time. It was awful. I just fell apart."

She continued quickly again with that warm, wry smile. "But my husband didn't. He was so strong. He talked with the doctors and knew what he had to do. He came to me and said it was time to say my good-byes. There was kindness in his eyes, and I knew what he said was true." Mrs. Burton paused for a moment, feeling again a pain more than forty years old. "So we said our good-byes and left.

"You know, it wasn't till years later that I found out about other things that went on that week. My husband had two spinster aunts that made all the funeral arrangements. They talked to the man at the funeral home, and they bought the plot. They got Susan the most beautiful dress, all covered with lace and ribbons and the tiniest little pearls you've ever seen. White. It was white, too. And they paid for it all."

As Mrs. Burton's story drew to a conclusion, I sat in stunned amazement. Though there are few things in life sadder than the death of a child, I did not leave her that day overwhelmed with sadness. Instead, I left amazed at *how* she told her sad story, the acts of kindness through which she saw it all. Kindness transformed her tragically sad story into a tale of true beauty. Thankfully, this dear, insightful woman had both the eyes to see such a marvelous transformation and the wisdom to speak its wonder into the lives of others such as mine.

Though the virtue of kindness is common to both genders, women tend to have a greater vision and inclination for performing simple acts of kindness. Because these ideas come so naturally to many women, we tend to dismiss the significance of such seemingly small acts of goodness. However, though we may diminish them, God does not.

AN ANCIENT WOMAN'S SOUL

In Ruth 1–4 we see that Ruth was not just kind; she was exceptionally kind. Her kindness reflected both her faith and her wisdom. It showed up in the most ordinary ways, reaping extraordinary results. Ruth's acts of kindness are a thread that unites and propels the story forward toward a surprisingly powerful conclusion.

Such simple kindness stands out in the context of the Old Testament. In a time when God's kingdom work was accomplished through kings and battles and wars whose intent was conquering foreign lands and peoples, Ruth stands apart both as a foreigner herself and as a woman who did the work of God in a different and uniquely feminine way.

Certainly both approaches reflect God's work in the world; though radically different, they are equally powerful. But through Ruth, our backward, upside-down, in-a-mirror womanly way shines forth.

The Root of Kindness

Don't urge me to leave you or to turn back from you. Where you go I will go, and where you stay I will stay. Your people will be my people and your God my God. Where you die I will die, and there I will be buried. May the Lord deal with me, be it ever so severely, if anything but death separates you and me. (1:16-17)

Though Ruth's choice to remain with Naomi was stated simply, the implications of this expression of kindness were great. For Ruth, it meant leaving her country, culture, religious tradition, and family of origin—everything familiar. As far as we know, she had never been to the land of Israel. My guess, though, is that she knew a bit about the culture, customs, and faith of the Jews because she invoked the Lord's name in her promise of loyalty to Naomi. She probably also had an idea of their penchant for the exclusion of foreigners.

As we noted in chapter 9, Ruth's decision was more intuitive than logical. Her vision for kindness was rooted in a gutfelt loyalty more than a specific vision of what life in this new land would bring. Faith more than sight moved her forward.

Naomi probably had her own set of concerns regarding Ruth's decision. Though the younger woman's physical strength and companionship would have been valuable, Naomi must have been concerned about the social acceptance of this Moabite daughter whom she loved. In the end, would she be an asset or a liability?

With so much uncertainty surrounding this choice, the only thing clear was Ruth's determination to go, a determination rooted in a heart full of kindness.

Respectful Initiative

Now Naomi had a relative on her husband's side, from the clan of Elimelech, a man of standing, whose name was Boaz.

And Ruth the Moabitess said to Naomi, "Let me go to the fields and pick up the leftover grain behind anyone in whose eyes I find favor."

Naomi said to her, "Go ahead, my daughter." (2:1-2)

What do you imagine Ruth felt when Naomi proclaimed her emptiness to her townspeople? Even though Ruth had left everything familiar behind her in order to accompany her mother-in-law back to Judah, Naomi's public conclusion was, "I went away full, but the LORD has brought me back empty" (1:21). Perhaps Ruth felt uncomfortable. Maybe she was so aware of Naomi's sense of loss that she did not take it personally at all. She might have been disturbed by Naomi's lack of acknowledgment that she, too, was widowed; she, too, had lost the immediate hope of children. In any case, we know that Ruth began her days in the land of Israel by initiating kindness toward Naomi.

As a woman overwhelmed with grief, Naomi was probably completely unconcerned with food. Somehow, Ruth had discovered the customary Jewish provision of gleaning in the fields behind the reapers. So she took the initiative.

It is significant that the author notes for us that Ruth asked Naomi for permission to go gather grain. Though Naomi seemed virtually incapacitated, Ruth continued to draw her out, honoring her with respect. She was careful not to disempower Naomi as she offered needed assistance. Her actions showed kindness by anticipating the time when Naomi, once again, would be the one able to care for others. Ruth was wise enough to know that acts of kindness without such respect are not truly kind.

Holy Curiosity

Just then Boaz arrived from Bethlehem and greeted the harvesters, "The Lord be with you!"

"The Lord bless you!" they called back.

Boaz asked the foreman of his harvesters, "Whose young woman is that?"

> *The foreman replied, "She is the Moabitess who came back from Moab with Naomi. She said, 'Please let me glean and gather among the sheaves behind the harvesters.' She went into the field and has worked steadily from morning till now, except for a short rest in the shelter."*
>
> *So Boaz said to Ruth, "My daughter, listen to me. Don't go and glean in another field and don't go away from here. Stay here with my servant girls. Watch the field where the men are harvesting, and follow along after the girls. I have told the men not to touch you. And whenever you are thirsty, go and get a drink from the water jars the men have filled."*
>
> *At this, she bowed down with her face to the ground. She exclaimed, "Why have I found such favor in your eyes that you notice me—a foreigner?" (verses 4-10)*

The trait of curiosity often gets a bad rap—as they say, "Curiosity killed the cat." Yet curiosity can be a very significant form of kindness. Consider Boaz's interest in Ruth. Clearly his intent was not to gossip or abuse but to bless. His simple inquiry seems to have been natural for him, giving him needed information for doing Ruth good.

Ruth's curiosity was much more of a risk. It is amazing that she dared to ask him for an explanation for his kindness. Think about the scene. She was a person with no social, political, or religious standing. She was lower than the low, deemed to be invisible in this culture.

Yet by her inquiry, she refused that spot of hiddenness and offered herself as a person, an individual with a mind and perceptions and curiosities. Her willingness to voice her curiosity presented her personhood as one worthy of consideration, relationship, and an answer.

Her offer of real relationship rather than personless servitude was a great kindness. The best we have to offer is *never* just our hands. We are not ministry machines. Again, acts of kindness without such a sense of personhood are not kind at all.

The Gift of Receiving

Boaz replied, "I've been told all about what you have done for your mother-in-law since the death of your husband—how you left your father and mother and your homeland and came to live with a people you did not know before. May the Lord repay you for what you have done. May you be richly rewarded by the Lord, the God of Israel, under whose wings you have come to take refuge."

"May I continue to find favor in your eyes, my lord," she said. "You have given me comfort and have spoken kindly to your servant—though I do not have the standing of one of your servant girls."

At mealtime Boaz said to her, "Come over here. Have some bread and dip it in the wine vinegar."

When she sat down with the harvesters, he offered her some roasted grain. She ate all she wanted and had some left over. As she got up to glean, Boaz gave orders to his men, "Even if she gathers among the sheaves, don't embarrass her. Rather, pull out some stalks for her from the bundles and leave them for her to pick up, and don't rebuke her." (verses 11-16)

How good are you at receiving compliments? If you are like most women, the answer would be, "Not very good." How about help? How easy is it for you to be on the receiving end of the ministry of others? Most of us struggle in this area, too.

Have you ever considered the very act of receiving as a kindness? This section of Scripture reflects many ways that Ruth offered the kindness within her soul through the choice to graciously receive the kindness of another. First, with her words, "May I continue to find favor," she simply accepted Boaz's compliment rather than seeking to refute or undo it.

Second, she spoke very specifically and vulnerably of the good impact his words had on her soul. She noted both his kindness and her own comfort. She not only let his words make a difference for her, but she let him know about it. She also noted her own social vulnerability, lower than that of even his servants, which highlighted his kindness to her.

Finally, she received his acts of kindness. She sat with the harvesters and ate until she was full. She made no attempt to diminish her need or hunger. There was no refusal of help, no hesitance to bless Boaz with the kindness of a gift graciously received.

Powerful Provision

So Ruth gleaned in the field until evening. Then she threshed the barley she had gathered, and it amounted to about an ephah. She carried it back to town, and her mother-in-law saw how much she had gathered. Ruth also brought out and gave her what she had left over after she had eaten enough.

Her mother-in-law asked her, "Where did you glean today? Where did you work? Blessed be the man who took notice of you!"

Then Ruth told her mother-in-law about the one at whose place she had been working. "The name of the man I worked with today is Boaz," she said.

"The Lord bless him!" Naomi said to her daughter-in-law. "He has not stopped showing his kindness to the living and the dead." She added, "That man is our close relative; he is one of our kinsman-redeemers."

Then Ruth the Moabitess said, "He even said to me, 'Stay with my workers until they finish harvesting all my grain.'"

Naomi said to Ruth her daughter-in-law, "It will be good for you, my daughter, to go with his girls, because in someone else's field you might be harmed."

So Ruth stayed close to the servant girls of Boaz to glean until the barley and wheat harvests were finished. And she lived with her mother-in-law. (verses 17-23)

155

Over the years, I have heard many women practice the art of self-depreciation I call "casserole bashing." When asked about their spiritual gifts or contribution to their community, they say apologetically, "Well, I just bake casseroles. That's all I know how to do." Somehow, I do not think that is how God sees those critically important acts of service.

In this part of our story, Ruth offered Naomi the equivalent of a casserole. Physical sustenance was the necessary beginning for many other kinds of "feeding" that went on in this exchange. Until those physical needs were met, other needs could never even rise to the surface to be addressed.

Notice the simple companionship of this scene. Ruth brought all the news of her day, sharing details about events and conversations. Through her experiences, she was feeding Naomi's need for social interaction. In the South, we call it the art and subtle gift of "visiting."

I love the way this section concludes: "And she lived with her mother-in-law." Naomi's profound grief undoubtedly made her feel half-dead. Ruth's presence was life itself. She brought life to her mother-in-law over and over through small but significant moments of provision. Never underestimate the potential power of a casserole.

Redemptive Cunning

One day Naomi her mother-in-law said to her, "My daughter, should I not try to find a home for you, where you will be well provided for? Is not Boaz, with whose servant girls you have been, a kinsman of ours? Tonight he will be winnowing barley on the threshing floor. Wash and perfume yourself, and put on your best clothes. Then go down to the threshing floor, but don't let him know you are there until he has finished eating and drinking. When he lies down, note the place where he is lying. Then go and uncover his feet and lie down. He will tell you what to do."

"I will do whatever you say," Ruth answered. So she went down to the threshing floor and did everything her mother-in-law told her to do. (3:1-6)

Naomi's plan was either a stroke of brilliance or a "senior" moment. Either way, it was both risky and risqué. Basically, she sent Ruth to seduce Boaz. There is no way to get around that fact. And Ruth agreed to the plan.

How do we look at such a moment? Is this an incident of one woman endangering another or a case of two intuitive, resourceful, and realistic women crafting a wise but risky plan? In this instance, it appears that however wise or ill-conceived the plan might have been, God protected Ruth and blessed the outcome.

Even as I struggle to make sense of the morality of this story, I somehow find myself learning from it. Like so many of her foremothers, Naomi had learned to work around the system to further her cause, a cause we eventually discover was also the cause of God. Rebekah and Rachel were both schemers for the good of God's kingdom. Tamar, too, worked around the stubborn will of her fearful father-in-law by using trickery. Rahab was a woman with her eye on God's blessing who achieved it using a bit of a questionable approach. In fact, three of these cunning women (Ruth, Rahab, and Tamar) are the *only* women mentioned by name in Matthew's genealogy of Jesus. Go figure. Perhaps God sees this kind of cunning as redemptive, the noble side of our feminine soul's destructive tendency toward manipulation. It seems to be a form of kindness God blesses for the sake of good.

The Kindness of Pursuit

When Boaz had finished eating and drinking and was in good spirits, he went over to lie down at the far end of the grain pile. Ruth approached quietly, uncovered his feet and lay down. In the middle of the night something startled the man, and he turned and discovered a woman lying at his feet.

"Who are you?" he asked.

"I am your servant Ruth," she said. "Spread the corner of your garment over me, since you are a kinsman-redeemer."

"The Lord bless you, my daughter," he replied. "This kindness is greater than that which you showed earlier: You have not run after the younger men, whether rich or poor. And now,

my daughter, don't be afraid. I will do for you all you ask. All my fellow townsmen know that you are a woman of noble character. Although it is true that I am near of kin, there is a kinsman-redeemer nearer than I. Stay here for the night, and in the morning if he wants to redeem, good; let him redeem. But if he is not willing, as surely as the Lord lives I will do it. Lie here until morning."

So she lay at his feet until morning, but got up before anyone could be recognized; and he said, "Don't let it be known that a woman came to the threshing floor."

He also said, "Bring me the shawl you are wearing and hold it out." When she did so, he poured into it six measures of barley and put it on her. Then he went back to town. (verses 7-15)

Notice Boaz's words: "This kindness is greater than that which you showed earlier: You have not run after the younger men, whether rich or poor." Apparently he saw Ruth's approach not as manipulation but as kindness. He considered it a compliment to be sought after by such a woman of excellence. He was pleasantly surprised that she saw his goodness, saw something attractive in him. Her feminine vision saw him holistically. She did not look at his age alone but at the whole of his person.

Ruth not only saw his goodness, but, even against the social norms of the day, she pursued it. From all we know of Boaz, he was a man of great standing in the community, as well as a kind man. It almost seems out of character that he would not have pursued Ruth in some way once the barley harvest was over and he no longer had opportunity to provide for her and Naomi. The readiness of the information about a closer kinsman might even indicate that he had done some initial investigation into the possibility.

His lack of initiative might have been what prompted Naomi's plan. His response lets us know he had not dared to assume Ruth's interest. Maybe her foreign status caused the hesitation. Perhaps this strong, usually assertive man found a place of fear and uncertainty in his relationship with Ruth. It is interesting to note that throughout the book of Ruth, the women are the ones who initiate new courses of action. In this instance, the force behind that initiative can clearly be labeled as kindness. Feminine action, feminine force.

The Transforming Power of Kindness

Then Boaz announced to the elders and all the people, "Today you are witnesses that I have bought from Naomi all the property of Elimelech, Kilion and Mahlon. I have also acquired Ruth the Moabitess, Mahlon's widow, as my wife, in order to maintain the name of the dead with his property, so that his name will not disappear from among his family or from the town records. Today you are witnesses!"

Then the elders and all those at the gate said, "We are witnesses. May the Lord make the woman who is coming into your home like Rachel and Leah, who together built up the house of Israel. May you have standing in Ephrathah and be famous in Bethlehem. Through the offspring the Lord gives you by this young woman, may your family be like that of Perez, whom Tamar bore to Judah."

So Boaz took Ruth and she became his wife. Then he went to her, and the Lord enabled her to conceive, and she gave birth to a son. The women said to Naomi: "Praise be to the Lord, who this day has not left you without a kinsman-redeemer. May he become famous throughout Israel! He will renew your life and sustain you in your old age. For your daughter-in-law, who loves you and who is better to you than seven sons, has given him birth."

Then Naomi took the child, laid him in her lap and cared for him. The women living there said, "Naomi has a son." And they named him Obed. He was the father of Jesse, the father of David. (4:9-17)

As he promised, Boaz acted quickly, faithfully, shrewdly. No lack of initiative or paralysis now. It is clear that his relationship with Ruth had breathed new life and hope into his future. The blessing of the townspeople clearly points to Ruth as the source of his hope for future blessing and significance in God's work in the world. Her kindness brought transformation to an old man.

The same is true for Naomi. Again, the townspeople clearly pointed to the kindness of Ruth as the source of new hope for her mother-in-law, this time in the form of the gift of a son. In the ancient world, the lines of heritage sometimes blended a bit in the midst of family. In terms of Jewish heritage, and possibly even physical parenting, Obed was as much Naomi's son as Ruth's. Note also that the very "ordinary" custom of levirate marriage that Naomi dismissed in chapter 1 as impossible was the very instrument God used to bring her redemption. The daughter-in-law who was invisible to her as she proclaimed her emptiness became a bigger blessing than seven sons. Isn't God amazing?

This is a story of ordinary people doing whatever it takes to make life work using whatever ordinary means—or questionable schemes—available to them. Though God is the unseen hand, ordinary kindness is the force that holds everything together and moves it forward. Surprisingly, this story that celebrates the ordinary ends with a very extraordinary twist. At the last minute, the author reveals to us that the characters in the story are intimately connected to royalty, King David. The good-news message of Jesus is foreshadowed once again: The ordinary becomes extraordinary, the weak become strong, the poor become rich, and simple kindness births God's kingdom.

That day in the hospital as I listened to Mrs. Burton's story, I also heard the glorious strains of that old gospel story. Through the kindness of those around her, God transformed a sad and tragic tale into a story of wonder, glory, and beauty. May our feminine souls never again underestimate the transforming power of kindness and its critically important place in kingdom work.

YOUR JOURNEY

For personal reflection and group discussion

1. Think about three expressions of kindness you have experienced from others. How did those acts impact you in the moment? Did they have a lasting effect of any kind? If so, describe it.

2. Recall moments of heartfelt loyalty in your life, times when you stuck with others or others stuck with you. Can you recall specific acts of kindness that flowed from those deep roots?

3. Have you ever been extended kindness in the context of disrespect? If so, describe the incident and your response.

4. Are there times when you have performed an act of kindness while seeking to hide your personhood? Imagine how a stronger sense of self might have enhanced the kindness the other person experienced.

5. On a scale of 1 to 10 (10 being very good), how good were you at receiving compliments or help offered by others this week? Describe the specific situations in as much detail as you can.

6. Are you a "casserole basher"? How can you affirm for yourself, other women, and your community the power of simple kindness?

7. Have you ever used redemptive cunning for the sake of good? Tell about the situation, your scheme, and the outcome.

8. What relationships in your life need the kindness of pursuit this week? Are there concerns such as social norms that make you hesitate to offer this form of kindness?

9. What words of affirmation and reward do you imagine God would want you to hear for the kindnesses you offered this week?

CHAPTER ELEVEN

Celebrating Our Complexity, Offering Our Wisdom

LADY WISDOM IN PROVERBS 31

In contrast to King Solomon's straightforward, simple wisdom in the bulk of the book, complex Lady Wisdom bookends Proverbs. When we as women own and speak our more complicated perspective into the world, we often find ourselves in tension with others. Representing wisdom as both feminine and complex, God affirms and celebrates our beneficial complexity.

To Consider . . .

Can you remember a time when you knew that offering your perspective would add complexity to a moment, so you held your tongue? Specifically, whom or what did you fear? In the end, were you pleased with your choice?

"YOU'VE got to be crazy! I can't believe how complicated you're making this whole thing. Can't we just get in the car and go?"

That was my husband's response to my to-do list a week before we left on vacation in the summer of 1987. And he was right. I was a little crazy. With three young children, ages six, three, and a newborn, it was pretty insane to go to the grocery store, much less take a two-week vacation driving from Texas to Minnesota and back! Sadly, at that point in my feminine spiritual journey, I was so completely unaware of my own personhood that I didn't even think about the fact that I had given birth less than three weeks earlier.

Crazy as I might have been to decide with my husband to take such a taxing vacation that summer, the complexity of my planning was very sane. Children need to eat. The more fast food and sugar, the worse the behavior, so I planned lunches and snacks on the road. They get bored in the car, so I bought small toys that I wrapped for daily surprises, borrowed others from friends, and adapted some of their own to work better in the car. Children need to run and move, so I carefully planned stops and lunch breaks at parks and zoos from Texas all the way to Minnesota. And all this on a budget.

My complexity of planning paid off. We had a wonderful trip with relatively few meltdowns. That is, except for me. When we got to my sister-in-law's house in Minnesota, I could hardly get out of bed. I could not figure out why my body was betraying me. It took a while to clue in to the fact that giving birth such a short time ago and nursing a baby through the night might be the reason. It seems that in all my fancy planning, I had forgotten myself.

Eventually recovering from that trip, I began to wonder about my penchant for complexity. Though I was pretty confident it had worked for good in the vacation-planning scenario (with the exception of forgetting myself), it was a matter of ongoing discussion in our marriage.

I was beginning to express my own thoughts and opinions more and more, and I did not necessarily like the problems it caused. My more complex perspective regularly complicated decision-making processes in the household. My more convoluted way of seeing things always seemed to, at least in the short run, cause trouble. Whether the issue was which relative to stay with at Christmas, a particular seating arrangement for a dinner party, or how much money to budget for a washing machine, my input always seemed to add a dimension of complexity. Still, it was the only way I *could* see things.

Three years ago, after years of struggle (in fact, I think it was over a decade later!), a moment of insight came as I was beginning a study on the book of Proverbs. Right away I loved the idea that wisdom is personified as a woman in the beginning and end of the book. But what really opened my eyes was Lady Wisdom's first cry in chapter 1:

> *Wisdom calls aloud in the street,*
> *she raises her voice in the public squares;*
> *at the head of the noisy streets she cries out,*
> *in the gateways of the city she makes her speech:*
> *"How long will you simple ones love your simple ways?*
> *How long will mockers delight in mockery*
> *and fools hate knowledge?" (verses 20-22)*

Did she say what I thought she said? Could it be that simple is not always better? That complexity is a part of—in fact, an essential element of—wisdom? Could it be that my complicated perspective is actually a gift from God to be celebrated and used, even at the expense of simplicity and efficiency? The more I studied Lady Wisdom, the more I heard her initial cry expounded.

AN ANCIENT WOMAN'S SOUL

For the sake of our scope here, we will look only at Proverbs 31. Though this is not technically a story, it is a description of an interesting character. This passage is often used as a laundry list of how to be an excellent wife. Many women have felt frustrated, overwhelmed, and even condemned by the passage.

Some scholars see it a bit differently: Lady Wisdom's voice ending this book as it began.[1] Wisdom's personification as a woman perhaps indicates our stronger feminine connection with wisdom. When we read this text as a description of Lady Wisdom rather than of the perfect wife, it offers challenges to both sexes.

One thing comes forth loud and clear: Lady Wisdom was complicated and proud of it! She had a rich, full, and varied life. She was also savvy enough to not forget herself in the middle of all that complexity. She has a lot to teach us all.

Grounded in Good

A wife of noble character who can find?
She is worth far more than rubies.
Her husband has full confidence in her
and lacks nothing of value.
She brings him good, not harm,
all the days of her life. (verses 10-12)

Wisdom's first descriptor is "noble character," or, as others translate it, "virtuous."[2] Though we tend to read that word as "righteous" or "morally proper," many interpret the word to mean "strong," even "forceful." We are talking about a woman of wisdom and impact—a woman who makes a difference in the world around her.

The word for *husband* in verse 11 could have the alternate meaning of "the one who possesses her."[3] It would read like this: "The one who possesses Lady Wisdom has full confidence in her and lacks nothing of value." Truly wise people know they are wise. Such calm and grounded self-assurance is far from arrogance. It is not independent of God but instead confidently assumes God's presence within. Wise people have ways of knowing that include and transcend our general view of knowledge. They have confidence in their perspective, intuition, and sufficiency. This trust in themselves has been hard-won through many experiences. Over years and years they have learned that wisdom will not let them down. They have learned to trust their gut.

A Picky Planner

She selects wool and flax
and works with eager hands.
She is like the merchant ships,
bringing her food from afar.
She gets up while it is still dark;
she provides food for her family
and portions for her servant girls.
She considers a field and buys it;
out of her earnings she plants a vineyard. (verses 13-16)

Wisdom is discerning. She does not choose the first thing that comes her way. She rejects the simple or easy way. Wisdom selects; she is picky. She goes to great lengths to find what she wants. She is an extra-effort gal—high maintenance, you might even say. Clearly, though, she is worth the trouble.

Even though she is choosy and willing to complicate the scene to get what she wants, she is not unnecessarily inefficient. She is a careful planner. Wisdom understands the specific needs and makes sure the provision is ready and appropriate. She is "in touch."

The word for *considers* could also be translated "devises." Though as women we often struggle to own our sinful manipulative tendencies, here they are redeemed into productive creativity. Wisdom initiates, evaluates, and designs a plan and then acts. Her discerning nature, an ability to bring many complex facets to such planning and decisions, is an essential element of her wisdom.

Strong and Satisfied

She sets about her work vigorously;
her arms are strong for her tasks.
She sees that her trading is profitable,
and her lamp does not go out at night. (verses 17-18)

Unlike me in my vacation scenario, Lady Wisdom does not forget herself. The NASB translates verse 17 as

She girds herself with strength
and makes her arms strong.

There is something very intentional about Lady Wisdom's strength. She actively makes choices that grow her being: body, mind, and soul. Not only is she not invisible to herself, but she is consciously working to strengthen herself.

Wisdom takes time out to "feel the moment." The word for *sees* actually means "tastes." She does not just blow past moments of achievement and success; she experiences them with great presence and intentionality. She savors her soul's satisfaction.

And it is that moment of goodness, *not* the drudgery of duty, that propels her into overtime. Wisdom is motivated organically, from the inside out. Notice throughout this passage the absence of duty, law, and obligation. Lady Wisdom is passionate, intrinsically inspired to "stay up late."

Balanced Compassion

In her hand she holds the distaff
and grasps the spindle with her fingers.
She opens her arms to the poor
and extends her hands to the needy. (verses 19-20)

There are many elements in this chapter that reflect tensions of difference, such as bringing food from afar *and* planning efficiently, or strengthening herself *and* staying up late. None are more obvious than the one in this section. Let the image form in your mind. First her hands "hold" and "grasp"; then those same hands "open" and "extend."

Wisdom necessitates the hard work of balancing competing demands. She is attentive to her "at home," "hands inward" responsibilities and at the same time addresses the "hands out" needs in the world around her. Balancing tensions such as these is always complicated. Wisdom chooses neither simplicity nor ease.

Beautifully Prepared

When it snows, she has no fear for her household;
for all of them are clothed in scarlet.
She makes coverings for her bed;
she is clothed in fine linen and purple. (verses 21-22)

Have you ever thought of the "nesting" instinct in women as an element of wisdom? Wisdom makes a nest for her household and herself. She provides the needed internal warmth with her lack of fear and the external warmth with clothes and bedding.

Ah, but not just *any* clothes and bedding. Like our feminine gender, wisdom knows the value of beauty. Again, she is fussy, refusing the less complicated solution. Unapologetically, she herself wears the finest clothes of all.

Well-Respected, Well-Connected

Her husband is respected at the city gate,
where he takes his seat among the elders of the land.
She makes linen garments and sells them,
and supplies the merchants with sashes. (verses 23-24)

Once again, read *husband* as "the one who possesses Lady Wisdom." Those who are wise are known and respected. Others, even leaders, seek their wisdom. Remember, these are not the "quick and easy answer" folks; rather, they make choices that have been proven over time.

In addition, wisdom is not afraid of a dose of worldly ambition. There is a practicality that does not insist that goodness be all about charity. Note that this is yet another tension in this passage. Wisdom knows that production and profit can be forces for good in the world. The business world is not the enemy but simply another arena for doing good.

Confidently Dignified

She is clothed with strength and dignity;
she can laugh at the days to come. (verse 25)

Let this image sink in for a moment. What does your image of Lady Wisdom, clothed in strength and dignity, look like? Whatever details you might imagine, one thing is for sure: She is the absolute opposite of a woman in hiding. She is substantial in presence. Though complex, the way of wisdom is not fragmented and fragile but whole and ripe. There is a solidness and straightness to her that comes from all aspects being gathered into a whole.

What does Lady Wisdom's laugh sound like? I imagine it as free, full, and easy. Wisdom is hopeful and optimistic about the future. Her laugh comes from her belly, rooted in her intuitive, seasoned, and trusted gut.

Articulate and Aware

She speaks with wisdom,
and faithful instruction is on her tongue.
She watches over the affairs of her household
and does not eat the bread of idleness. (verses 26-27)

Lady Wisdom has clearly found her voice and offers her perspective freely. Again, we get the sense of an inside-out movement. She speaks what she knows to be true, not what others want to hear. Wisdom refuses negative censors, within or without.

Though clearly she is self-aware, Lady Wisdom is not self-focused. Again, a tension. She is alert and aware of the needs around her and works to meet those needs, investing her time well rather than in the trivia of laziness.

Centered and Celebrated

Her children arise and call her blessed;
  her husband also, and he praises her:
"Many women do noble things,
  but you surpass them all."
Charm is deceptive, and beauty is fleeting;
  but a woman who fears the Lord is to be praised.
Give her the reward she has earned,
  and let her works bring her praise at the city gate. (verses 28-31)

The word in verse 29 translated here as "noble" is actually the same word we began with: *virtuous*. Remember, it can be interpreted as "strong, forceful." This repetition reminds us that wisdom is a force in the world, perhaps the greatest force of all.

This greatness comes from the fact that wisdom is a force centered in God. Wisdom, in all her variety and complexity, is grounded in reverence for God. Thus far, we have been told of things she does *not* fear: snow and the future. We know that wisdom sees through the temporary points of power so many around her rely upon: charm (being favored by others) and external beauty. Only now do we see her compass, her internal reference point, her guiding fear, her center. It is as if, having watched her behavior from afar these many verses, we are allowed a glimpse into her very heart.

This inward glimpse is sandwiched between the very outward-looking praise of those who know her best, her children and her husband. With this reading, we might define the children of Lady Wisdom as the fruits that wisdom produces in our lives. Those actions and choices that come from our wisdom give credit to the wisdom within. This metaphorical reading is echoed in a more direct statement in verse 31: "Her works bring her praise." Wisdom has earned her reward. The evidence is abundant, within and without, and speaks loudly on her behalf.

Even as we celebrate, it is important to remember that this has not been an easy path for Lady Wisdom. Nevertheless, she has not given in to simplicity along the way. Just as we were assured in the beginning, so now this celebration echoes this assurance once again: Complex and troublesome though it may be, wisdom is indeed worthy of the extra effort. In Lady Wisdom, our backward, upside-down, in-a-mirror world as women suddenly is the norm, the expected, the way of wisdom, even when it complicates life for those around us.

Not long ago I was telling the story of my feminine spiritual journey to a new friend, Karen. She was somewhat appalled as she began to see the complexity my growth had brought to our family life. As she listened, she felt acutely the cost of engaging two equal perspectives, my husband's and my own, affecting everything from budgeting to vacation plans to when we have sex to a move to Seattle. Karen was just beginning, at age forty-five, to become more aware of her own voice and soul, but she was very hesitant to speak her perspective, even within her own household. Her reluctance centered on the concern that she knew she would be causing "trouble" for others. Her struggle to accept and embrace the God-ordained complexity of her wisdom was a major challenge to her spiritual growth as a woman and potentially stifled the good God intended for her as one called to serve from the fullness of her feminine soul.

Lady Wisdom cries out, "How long will you simple ones love your simple ways?" She challenges us as women to value our complex perspectives. Though this is not an easy path, it is the one God has called us to live. May we as women remember Lady Wisdom as we struggle with our feminine souls' more complicated way of seeing the world.

YOUR JOURNEY

For personal reflection and group discussion

1. Describe a wise woman you know well and respect. What in her life echoes what you have learned about Lady Wisdom?

2. Have you ever been accused of complicating a situation or discussion? Recall the details of the scene and the way you felt about it.

3. Recall a time when you were choosy about something. Do you see that choosiness as a part of your wisdom? Why or why not? How did those around you regard your tendency to be selective?

4. What choices have you made this week to intentionally strengthen yourself? Have there been any moments of soul satisfaction that you chose to enhance with celebration or avoid with neglect?

5. How well do you generally negotiate the tension between "hands inward" and "hands outward" service? What would those closest to you say?

6. List some of your "nesting" activities this week. Spend a few minutes connecting them in your mind to God's description of Lady Wisdom. Do you see them any differently?

7. Describe in detail or sketch your imagined picture of Lady Wisdom, clothed in strength and dignity, smiling at the future.

8. How do you feel about the idea of offering your wisdom to others? Are you hesitant? Neglectful? Afraid? Free? Too free?

9. Describe as best you can your personal internal compass, reference point, center. How is that center reflected on an average day in your life?

10. What new choices will you make this week in pursuit of becoming a wise woman who makes a difference in the world around her?

CHAPTER TWELVE

Maximizing Our Impact, Offering Our Language

THE WOMAN WITH THE ALABASTER JAR IN MARK 14:1-11

Women often love and care for others in memorable and powerful ways using few, if any, words. We know how to speak a language without words. Like the woman with the alabaster jar, we have a special gift for beauty making, using environment, experiences, and images to touch and heal the most tender parts of hurting hearts. By projecting the retelling of this story into the future life of the church, Jesus puts this uniquely feminine ministry on par with Peter's word-oriented confession.

To Consider . . .

Science has shown for years that we are significantly impacted by our physical surroundings. Recall a time when your environment had an effect on you, for good or for ill.

WHEN I arrived in the hospital room, I found Mrs. Ingram alone, her husband downstairs for a treatment. Sparse rays of low afternoon sun entered through a partially closed curtain, bathing the room with a gentle light. After introducing myself, I sat down in a chair facing Mrs. Ingram, who had been napping briefly on a small sofa. As we visited, she told me the story of her husband's recent decline in health and poor prognosis. Her face and voice reflected a strong sense of sadness and a deep weariness. She informed me that they were going home later that day. We spoke briefly about pending decisions and paperwork to be done, but soon such legal issues became more the "rabbit trail" than the point of our conversation.

As often happens when sad stories are shared, one grief began to connect to others. The conversation led to talk of other experiences of loss in Mrs. Ingram's life. She told me about caring for her father, bedridden with cancer twenty years before. "Three years in bed and no bed sores," she offered proudly, finding some goodness to celebrate. Mrs. Ingram mentioned that she had hung a picture of Jesus on the wall opposite her father's bed. She spoke slowly, deliberately, eyes lowered, her body motionless and weighed down.

Death had become a part of her daily life again a few years later when her sister was also diagnosed with cancer. As I listened intently, it was not difficult to see the beauty in Mrs. Ingram's sad story. She described in vivid detail the holy space she had created for her sister: the light blue walls, the large windows with curtains always open to the natural light. She recounted how she had splurged on expensive linens, especially soft.

She talked about keeping fresh flowers in a vase near her sister's bed: "Daisies. Her favorite." Mrs. Ingram had even taken a course in reflexology to be able to give her sister "the best foot rubs known in all womankind." And the ever-present picture of Jesus oversaw it all.

Her narrative continued as she told of her sister's dying moments in the same room, same bed, from the same disease. "She wasn't a religious woman, but we'd called the preacher out, and they talked." Suddenly her shoulders straightened. The pace and energy in her words increased. "I knew she was dying. She hadn't talked in days. I was holding her, and all of a sudden, she raised up, reached for that picture, and said out loud, 'Jesus!'" Mrs. Ingram's voice and expression were now bright and animated, very different from moments before. As she spoke, a smile began to dawn on her lips. "I was so afraid she was going to fall out of bed." Imagining the sight, she almost giggled. "She was a big woman. I couldn't have done anything if she had." She became quiet, her face fully open toward me. "Then she laid back down against me and took her last breath." We sat together for a long time in awed silence.

As I listened, I made a few gentle inquiries, seeking to highlight for Mrs. Ingram the healing goodness and beauty of the experience she had so carefully crafted for her dying sister. We reflected a bit longer, savoring each detail of her memory. Eventually, we spoke of the comforting power of beauty. A tranquil softness settled over Mrs. Ingram.

Suddenly, out of the beautiful memories and stillness came body-shaking tears and a soulful wail, "I'm taking him home to that picture of Jesus."

Several minutes later when her voice returned, Mrs. Ingram's demeanor had once again shifted. Almost energetically, she began to create, offering up freshly born hopes about how this next chapter of grief in her life would be written. At once, she was present to both her pain and her desire. She spoke again of the bed and the picture and a healing ointment she had recently received from a television evangelist. She had forgotten about the balm until this visionary moment. She could not remember what they called it, but she excitedly told me she knew right where it was at home. Her tear-stained face glowed, restored and inspired for the healing work ahead.

Experiences of beauty create powerful contexts in which healing begins. They offer new hope for present pain. Remember the story of the prodigal son? After who knows how long a time of destruction and decline, culminating in desperate dining among pigs, his restoration began the moment he remembered the beauty of home.

Experiences of beauty often open parts of our hearts that words have failed to touch. Not long after I met Mrs. Ingram, I began a support group for pastors' wives in my town. Emboldened by the new wisdom I had been given from that encounter, I purposely chose to rely on environment and experiences of beauty more than words in this new ministry endeavor. We met monthly under the title of "Linger Longer Lunch," and I worked for days prior to each meeting seeking to craft each detail—the invitations, flowers, table setting, and food—into a healing experience of beauty for these women. I intentionally avoided any prescribed focus or agenda for conversation, though certainly conversation was welcome and abundant. Time after time, I was amazed at the power of these experiences. More than once, a woman would break into tears simply at the sight of the beautifully welcoming table.

Though our feminine souls are generally gifted in this wordless language of ministry, we often diminish the significance and power of this precious gift. We are aware of our ability, yet we fail to recognize and develop its power. Beauty making, one of our powerful tools for God's kingdom, remains imprisoned by our lack of vision, hidden even from us. Yet once again, what we may have failed to notice, Jesus did not. In the story of His encounter with the woman with the alabaster jar, He invites us not only to see and own this powerful gift but also to let it shine for all to celebrate.

AN ANCIENT WOMAN'S SOUL

This story in Mark 14:1-11 is one of several accounts of a woman anointing Jesus. The stories differ in a few details, and one seems to be set closer to the beginning of Jesus' ministry than the end. Though we do not know how many times this experience actually happened, scholars generally agree that the core message of these stories is the same and is one of "messianic importance."[1] For the sake of simplicity, we will focus on Mark's account.

Dangerous Times

Now the Passover and the Feast of Unleavened Bread were only two days away, and the chief priests and the teachers of the law were looking for some sly way to arrest Jesus and kill him. "But not during the Feast," they said, "or the people may riot." (verses 1-2)

What a tumultuous time in the life of Christ! It is difficult to imagine all that Jesus must have been experiencing and feeling as these events close to His death unfolded. He had just been the recipient of resounding praise as He entered Jerusalem. Yet internally, He was ever aware that His betrayal and death were fast approaching. The fickleness of the public and the threatening schemes of the Jewish leadership must have been an ever-present burden to His soul.

Repeatedly, He spoke to His disciples about His pending death. Repeatedly, He found them arguing about who would be His right-hand man in the new political order. Not only was He in pain, but He was also alone. I do not get a sense that He was afraid, but I do get a sense that He was disturbed, in grief over the city, in pain over the coming events, wrestling with the plans of God. Jesus was urgent in His teaching of the Twelve, seeking to focus on the need of the moment.

Bold Beauty Making

While he was in Bethany, reclining at the table in the home of a man known as Simon the Leper, a woman came with an alabaster jar of very expensive perfume, made of pure nard. She broke the jar and poured the perfume on his head. (verse 3)

As we have similarly noted in previous chapters, though the record of this woman's loving act is simply stated, it was not a simple choice for her to make. It is generally taught that the perfume was an extravagantly generous offering, probably her entire "retirement account," given freely in a moment of great passion. The abundance and lack of a measured approach is a critical part of the beauty of this moment.

The gift was not only generous; it was also very sensual. Notice the words of the passage: *alabaster, perfume of pure nard, broke, poured.* These words engage the imagination of our eyes, nose, ears, and touch. John's account says that the fragrance filled the room. Also note the absence of spoken words. It is as if they would only have distracted from fully absorbing the intensity of such an experience. This was a moment of overwhelming beauty, engaging the body and the heart.

This woman's actions were very bold. Though anointing of the head is common in Scripture, for this act to be done by a woman was radical. Not only that, but she did it publicly in the presence of several men. Unmeasured generosity, overwhelming sensuality, unconventional behavior. This was a shout, not a whisper.

Even still, I think the most radical thing about this moment is that the creature was ministering to the Creator. Jesus actively received the nurturing care and comforting ministry of this unnamed woman. That powerful, radical ministry came in the form of a deeply impacting experience of beauty: The jar broke, the oil flowed, and fragrance saturated the air.

A Harsh Rebuke

Some of those present were saying indignantly to one another, "Why this waste of perfume? It could have been sold for more than a year's wages and the money given to the poor." And they rebuked her harshly. (verses 4-5)

A part of reading the power of a moment is to look at the response it draws from the opposition. It is not unusual, though it is generally unexpected, for beauty to draw such a venomous response.

Somewhere along the way in our Christian tradition, the idea of being a good steward has become equated with the idea of being practical. Certainly a case can be made that God is not always practical. After all, God made winding rivers, not straight highways. God built feast after feast into the Jewish calendar. And there was certainly nothing "practical" or "measured" about the ornamentation on the temple. The gospel itself is the most telling expression of God's "foolishness." Why go to such an extreme expense to save a people such as us?

Sadly, in the name of practicality disguised as good stewardship, many beauty-making moments are diminished, negated, or condemned even before they come to be. We too quickly compromise on our vision for a beautiful piece of stained glass for the sanctuary, our desire to serve prime rib just once at a dinner party, or our advocacy for that soft, white wool rug for our office. We hesitate to spend time or money on a massage or to speak up in favor of selecting the more lovely retreat setting for the annual women's retreat because it is an hour from home. As we see and begin to own the God-ordained power of beauty, our decisions will likely reflect that altered vision.

A part of beginning to own the powerful contribution of beauty making is to also own the strength of the opposition to it. Sometimes the opposition is wisely practical, but sometimes it is not. We cannot expect beauty making to be smooth sailing. Evil always opposes the glory of God. Any expression of beauty as a reflection of that glory is no exception to that rule. Some will seek not only to avoid this form of love but also to actively destroy it.

These harsh and visionless voices are not just outside us, as in this story. Many times they reign within. They seek to quench the beauty-making Spirit of God. They seek to deny the powerfully important and loving impact of moments such as these. When beauty draws the fire of the enemy, we are tempted to join the ranks of that enemy, avoiding it at all costs. Jesus acted quickly to make sure that did not happen here.

Helped by Beauty

"Leave her alone," said Jesus. "Why are you bothering her? She has done a beautiful thing to me. The poor you will always have with you, and you can help them any time you want. But you will not always have me." (verses 6-7)

Hear those words again. They are words for you, oh beauty makers of the world. In the face of those voices—including our own inner voices—that accuse, Jesus says (in effect), "You go, girl!" Jesus calls this woman's bold act a "beautiful thing." No other descriptors are needed.

He also leaves us with the sense that just as the poor can be helped in the future, the future He would not have on earth, this experience was helpful to Him. Again, we note that Jesus was acutely aware of His pending death. How sad that in this powerful and rare moment of receiving comfort, He had to move so quickly to the protection of this woman and the rebuke of her accusers.

Though there was no time to savor this experience in that moment, the overwhelming fragrance of such a precious perfume, especially in such an unimaginable abundance, must have lingered with Jesus for many days. (Unlike many of us, Jesus did not bathe every day.) My guess is that this fragrance was the only point of comfort and goodness Jesus carried with Him into the garden and the courts, before Pilate, and while He was beaten. The fragrance on His head mixed with the bloody crown of thorns. Perhaps it even endured to the cross. Jesus was indeed helped by this moment of beauty.

Doing What She Could

"She did what she could. She poured perfume on my body beforehand to prepare for my burial." (verse 8)

For a long time, Jesus had been talking plainly to His twelve disciples about His death, but we have no indication that they heard or accepted what He was saying. I can only imagine how much more difficult their lack of understanding made this moment for their Teacher. Yet someone had heard. Jesus was not the only One in the room who felt the weight of the coming suffering.

We do not really know how much this woman understood: death, burial, resurrection? Or what she imagined the fruit of her actions to be: worship, comfort, preparation for burial? I hear in Jesus' words that she would have liked to have done more. Maybe she wanted to save Him from His suffering. Perhaps she wanted to make Him politically powerful, above the Romans. Or possibly she wanted to foil somehow the religious leaders of the day who were so bent on His destruction. Yet she had no power in those arenas: physically, socially, religiously. Whatever her grief might have been regarding what she could *not* do, it did not stop her from doing what she could.

As we can see from this side of the Resurrection, what she could do was exactly what was needed the most. Many people in extreme duress have a difficult time focusing mentally. Words of comfort often roll off their beings, unable to be absorbed. The same, however, is not true of experiences. These experiential, physical messages of comfort reach where words cannot go. They linger in crevices of memory that can no longer hold words. Comfort, companionship, and healing beauty were what Jesus needed the most. I am so thankful she did what she could.

Memorable Impact

> *"I tell you the truth, wherever the gospel is preached throughout the world, what she has done will also be told, in memory of her."*
> *(verse 9)*

In the New Testament, Jesus projects only two specific moments directly into the life of the yet-to-be-born church. Interestingly, both moments carry the same message: Jesus is the Anointed One of God. Same message, different modes of communication, both memorable. One is Peter's great confession in Matthew 16:15-19:

> *"But what about you?" [Jesus] asked. "Who do you say I am?"*
> *Simon Peter answered, "You are the Christ, the Son of the living God."*
> *Jesus replied, "Blessed are you, Simon son of Jonah, for this was not revealed to you by man, but by my Father in heaven. And I tell you that you are Peter, and on this rock I will build my church, and the gates of Hades will not overcome it. I will give you the keys of the kingdom of heaven; whatever you bind on earth will be bound in heaven, and whatever you loose on earth will be loosed in heaven."*

Note a few things about this passage. First, only men are involved. Second, the confession is words alone, no action or experience of the senses. A significant part of the story is Peter's renaming—again, a focus on the power of words. Third, Jesus immediately reminds Peter that it is not man (Peter included) that discovered this truth, but it was revealed by a source beyond. It is as if Jesus is trying to nip in the bud Peter's tendency to overestimate his sense of personhood.

Contrast this with the equally weighty but very different passage in Mark 14:1-11. First, this instance involves an unnamed woman. The focus is on the action or experience, what she has done. Second, though words are involved in the transfer of the story, they are just that: *story* words that translate a sensual and concrete image rather than a concept or precept like Peter's confession. Third, Jesus elevates this woman's sense of self rather than seeking to counter or diminish it. The story will be told "in memory of *her*."

Again, though we in the church have missed the differences in masculine and feminine spirituality, God has not. Feel the weight of His concrete affirmation of this woman and her beauty-making gift. Never, never doubt the power of such moments for the good of God's kingdom in the world.

A Radical Reaction

> *Then Judas Iscariot, one of the Twelve, went to the chief priests to betray Jesus to them. They were delighted to hear this and promised to give him money. So he watched for an opportunity to hand him over. (verses 10-11)*

Judas, as well as Jesus, was impacted by this pervasively powerful experience. His lack of ability to understand or agree with Jesus' support of this woman's actions further alienated him from the One he once called Teacher. It seems that he knew once and for all that he and Jesus did not have the same vision for the coming kingdom. Jesus' response to this beauty-making moment had made that clear.

Moments of beauty like this one are not trivial; they are an important part of the gospel being lived out in our world. They communicate well, draw enemy fire, and change lives. Just as this woman helped Jesus long ago, we, too, can use beauty making to help His body still on earth. Let us learn to maximize our feminine souls' effective service by living well our language of beauty making. May it also be said of each of us, "She has done a beautiful thing to me."

YOUR JOURNEY

For personal reflection and group discussion

1. Describe the most beautiful environment you can imagine.

2. Describe a wordless experience of nurturing that you either gave or received.

3. Imagine the many dimensions of Jesus' turmoil during the days before His arrest. Record as many elements of His struggles as you can.

4. Recall and recount a time when you ministered to another person through the language of beauty making.

5. On a scale of 1 to 10 (10 being very powerful and important), how do you generally rank beauty-making moments alongside other forms of ministry?

6. Can you remember a time when you were rebuked (internally or externally) for investing in beauty? Describe the situation and your response. Read again Jesus' words in your defense.

7. Can you imagine new ways to use your beauty-making gifts to help Jesus and/or His body here on earth?

8. Have there been moments when you underestimated or trivialized the power of beauty making, feeling that it was not enough in a moment of great need?

9. Have you ever backed away from beauty, fearing the negative response of others?

10. How does this story change your ideas about powerful service to God?

CONCLUSION

A Healing Revolution

To acknowledge the validity of our feminine spiritual journey is to open ourselves up to grief, revolutionary change, and greater glory.

~

SOON after turning forty-five, I was sensing another shift brewing in my life. I decided to give myself the gift of a week at a monastery in Wisconsin. Because my local flight had been delayed by fog, as I arrived in Houston, I was eager to find my connection. The agent at the gate was busy with others, so I ventured farther into the terminal and quickly found a screen. When I did not see my flight among the options, I began to panic.

Waffling between moving farther down the concourse or going back to the gates I had just passed, I decided to opt for the only agent I could spot who was not already occupied with another customer—an agent at the empty counter of another airline. I am sure my budding panic was all over my face as I walked toward the middle-aged attendant.

To my utter amazement, as I approached, he said, "Are you Janet?" Now, this was Houston Intercontinental Airport. I had chosen the counter at random. And I was not wearing a name tag. "Yes, but . . ." was all I could get out as I glimpsed the marquee, which did indeed show the city of my destination. But this was the wrong airline. I put my ticket in his confidently outstretched hand and tried to gather my thoughts to tell him why this could not be right.

Without responding to my confusion, he smiled broadly and said sincerely, "We've been waiting for you." Having finished with my ticket, he handed it back to me and guided me quickly onto the Jetway. Only then did I notice, in oh-so-small letters beneath the boldface Continental name on my ticket, that this flight would be operated by another airline!

Still rapt in amazement, I hurried onto the plane. As he walked behind me, I heard him speak into his radio, "Well, we've got Janet, and we're on our way." I will never forget the strong, joyfully confident lilt in his voice, entirely void of anxiety or frustration. He was amused by my confusion but not the least bit dismissive of me. There was something awesome and wonderfully infectious about that moment.

As I settled into my seat, I felt as if I had just heard a message directly from God. His words and voice echoed in my soul: "Well, we've got Janet, and we're on our way." Somehow I knew those words were naming my coming soul shift.

It had taken me all of forty-five years to locate myself, to find Janet. Not that the journey was over; it was simply complete enough to be "on our way." It was complete enough to begin to tell my story and offer my good news to others. I was immediately tempted to ridicule myself for taking so long to locate myself. But that shame and accusation simply did not fit with the lilting voice of the announcer. As far as God was concerned, I was right on time. And so I began to write this book.

In a faith tradition that was initially founded on the simple testimony of a small band of Jesus' disciples, our personal stories are given great weight. In one sense, the words you have read in this book are just that: simply my story, my good news, my individual perspective on life and Scripture. In another sense, these conclusions are nothing short of revolutionary. I have wondered at times if I should stamp a big red Danger label on the front of this book. If we take seriously the idea that women are spiritually unique, different in significant ways from men, the implications for the church will be enormous.

First, we will be called into mourning for the pain of misunderstanding throughout centuries of church history. Over the years, both men and women have lost much. To acknowledge the validity of these words is to recognize that the absence of honoring the feminine soul's unique spirituality is a loss for us all. Even as I have spoken frankly and directly about the pain women have experienced in relationship and in the church, the reality is that both genders have sinned and both have suffered. As we have said, our sinful patterns and contributions to this tragedy may look very different; nevertheless, we are equally accountable for sustaining these old grievous habits. As is almost always true, real transformation in the lives of individual men and women and the corporate church will come through the door of grief.

Second, our grief will lead us to massive systematic change. Adding the tension of a second voice, especially one that holds a more complex perspective on the world, will take huge amounts of effort and negotiation. Whatever the decision-making or governmental structure of a community, we will need to make decisions differently in churches, being careful that both male and female voices are heard, in order to have a more complete sense of God's leading. Sermons and Sunday school curriculum will reflect new complexities. The entire arena of biblical feminine spirituality needs much more exploration and scholarly reflection. The insights contained in this book have barely scratched the surface. The to-do list is endless, and the cost will be high.

Finally, as significant and problematic as these changes will be, I am convinced that they will pale in comparison to the enormous benefit the kingdom of God will experience if we dare to acknowledge gender-different spirituality. If women confront the destructive patterns within their feminine souls and choose healing, they will be freer than ever to grow and serve. If the church learns to wisely and specifically foster the growth of women, they will soar. Contrary to the false notion that strong women make weak men, I believe this feminine revolution will only serve to enhance us all. If we as a community become mindful and appreciative of uniquely feminine gifts, we will all experience the greater glory of God. As we live out the pattern God intended, maximizing both difference and equality, we will be blessed in ways we can only begin to imagine.

Even as I hope and pray for such a revolution, my primary passion continues to be for individual women. Culture shifts take time. True freedom and love are experienced only on a heart-to-heart basis.

Not long ago I was introduced to Melody when we shared a room at a retreat center near my home in Texas. Just finishing up the final months of a medical residency program at a nearby hospital, she had come for a few days of reflection.

As we visited one long, quiet winter evening, I found the thirty-year-old woman's story intriguing. All her life Melody had wanted to be a doctor. She had worked tirelessly for years and years and years toward her goal. She had labored to gain the respect of her professors and peers. Her determination and amazing intellect had brought her significant success. At the top of her class, she had begun to entertain job offers from around the country. Such employment possibilities allowed her to begin to envision the next season of her life. In a few short months, she would be a full-fledged MD. All the expected external transitions were going smoothly. The same could not be said of Melody's internal world.

Melody told me that over the last year as her responsibilities at the hospital had begun to wane, the pace of her life had slowed a bit. In the stillness, quite unexpectedly, disquiet over this long-settled path began to surface from somewhere deep inside her soul. Foreign longings began to erupt. She had come away for this retreat in hopes of better identifying the substance of her inner turmoil.

In the ever-so-slight pause of the last year, a new woman, a burgeoning sense of Melody's long-ignored feminine soul, had begun to make herself known. Though many strong and logical voices played on in Melody's head, begging her to ignore these internal yearnings, Melody was wise enough to know that she dare not.

As I listened, she poured out beautiful images of the life she was beginning to imagine. She spoke of a profound desire to birth and parent children. She envisioned well-spent hours making mud pies with her progeny. She wanted to garden and cook supper each night. She talked about how critical simply spending time together with her husband was for her marriage, of how she valued their relationship, having almost lost it at one point in her education. Melody also voiced a deeply held sense of spirituality, a part of her life she definitely wanted to incorporate into her medical practice. She spoke of her personal need for time alone, for beauty, for retreat.

Melody began to recognize that through the years of busyness and the constant demands of medical school, internship, and residency, she had lost track of her feminine soul. Though she had grown as a woman of wisdom through her various experiences, she had never stopped to recognize how she had changed. Her shifting soul had been overshadowed by the unrelenting demands of her goal. She had no language for these erupting awarenesses. They seemed to have no place in her current world, to be almost incompatible with it. Somewhere along the way, Melody had lost touch with the most essential parts of her feminine soul, a deficit she was beginning to grieve for the first time.

As she continued to speak that evening, Melody voiced fears about whether negotiating her feminine soul within herself, much less communicating her unique career desires to a potential employer, was possible. She expressed anxiety about the loss of her hard-won respect among her peers. She knew they would not understand this shift. She also knew her previously imagined future would no longer work. What she did not know was whether or not she would have the courage to let go of such long-held and hard-won goals.

Throughout our conversation, I continued to affirm the complexity of her life and applaud her courage. Few women allow questions of this magnitude to emerge from their souls or their lips. Even fewer choose to honor them with some quiet time away. I also shared with her my own feminine journey and a few of the stories you have just read.

As she talked, Melody's own certainty about her feminine soul increased. My affirmation was clearly a secondary source of encouragement. She was speaking her own life into being, gathering all those parts of her self that had been exiled from her consciousness for so long. Though we did not resolve anything about her future that long winter evening, Melody left that conversation more whole, more at peace, and more confident that somehow she was headed in a good direction. With much negotiation ahead of her, she knew one thing with certainty: Whatever the cost, she wanted never again to give up any part of her distinctively feminine soul.

For most of us, as for Melody, our greatest struggles will be within. I pray that a healing revolution will take place in your heart. I pray that in these pages, you have experienced being specifically known and fully loved by God. I pray that you will celebrate your feminine soul just as God does. I pray that the freedom, affirmation, and growth you have tasted here will take root in your life and bear fruit into the lives of other women and the church at large. Inspired by our surprising mentors of old, may each of us allow the glory of God to shine freely, brilliantly, and beautifully through our feminine souls.

NOTES

Dedication

1. International Commission of English in the Liturgy (ICEL), *The Canticles: A Faithful and Inclusive Rendering from the Hebrew and Greek into Contemporary English Poetry, Intended Primarily for Communal Song and Recitation* (Chicago: Liturgy Training Publications, 1996), 5.

Chapter Four: Giving Up Words, Daring to Be Silent

1. Catherine Clark Kroeger and Mary J. Evans, *The IVP Women's Bible Commentary* (Downers Grove, IL: InterVarsity, 2002), 599.

Chapter Seven: Living God's Call, Growing in Groundedness and Confidence

1. Francis Brown, S. R. Driver, and C. A. Briggs, *Hebrew and English Lexicon of the Old Testament* (Oxford: Clarendon Press, n.d.), 726; Claus Westermann, *Genesis 12–26*, vol. 2, (Minneapolis: Augsburg, 1985), 281.

2. C. F. Keil and F. Delitzsch, *Commentary on the Old Testament*, vol. 1, *The Pentateuch* (Grand Rapids, MI: Eerdmans, 1978), 228–229.

Chapter Eight: Embracing Our Vulnerability, Growing in Strength

1. Matthew Henry, *Matthew Henry's Commentary on the Whole Bible*, vol. 5, *Matthew to John* (McLean, VA: MacDonald Publishing Company, n.d.), 497.

Chapter Eleven: Celebrating Our Complexity, Offering Our Wisdom

1. *The Expositor's Bible Commentary*, vol. 5, *Psalms–Song of Songs* (Grand Rapids, MI: Zondervan, 1991), 1128–1129.

2. Robert Young, *Young's Analytical Concordance to the Bible* (Grand Rapids, MI: Eerdmans, 1975), 1026.

3. Young, 505.

Chapter Twelve: Maximizing Our Impact, Offering Our Language

1. Catherine Clark Kroeger and Mary J. Evans, *The IVP Women's Bible Commentary* (Downers Grove, IL: InterVarsity, 2002), 570–571.

ABOUT THE AUTHOR

Janet Davis refers to herself as "one who gathers stories." Through her experiences in a wide variety of Christian traditions, she has spoken with many hundreds of women about their personal experience of the Christian life. Whether in the grocery store, hospital, Bible studies, or within her own circle, she has listened well to the cries of women's hearts.

As Janet began to see themes within these gathered stories of a woman's experience of God, she began to question some of the assumptions the church has made for generations: chiefly, the assumption that spirituality is unisex. Exploring popular and feminine spirituality led her to see how they often present approaches to spiritual growth that are more effective for women. Hesitating to believe that what was true in life experience would not also be found in Scripture, Janet's love of Scripture led her back to the Text—specifically, to the stories of women in Scripture. The wisdom and healing she personally discovered in those stories she now offers other women.

With her Masters degree in Spiritual Nurture from Western Seminary-Seattle (now Mars Hill Graduate School), Janet works as a spiritual director, retreat speaker, and writer. She and her husband of thirty plus years, Bob, appreciate any time they can spend with their four grown children, Bobby, Jenna, Joel, and Betsy.

She also maintains a website at janetdavisonline.com